GLOBETROTTER™

Th

SING

HELEN OON

NEW
HOLLAND

GLOBETROTTER™

First edition published in 2005
by New Holland Publishers (UK) Ltd
London • Cape Town • Sydney • Auckland
10 9 8 7 6 5 4 3 2 1

website: www.newhollandpublishers.com

Garfield House, 86 Edgware Road
London W2 2EA
United Kingdom

80 McKenzie Street
Cape Town 8001
South Africa

14 Aquatic Drive
Frenchs Forest, NSW 2086
Australia

218 Lake Road
Northcote, Auckland
New Zealand

Distributed in the USA by
The Globe Pequot Press, Connecticut

ISBN 1 84330 837 1

Publishing Manager (UK): Simon Pooley
Publishing Manager (SA): Thea Grobbelaar
DTP Cartographic Manager: Genené Hart

Editor: Thea Grobbelaar
Cover design: Nicole Engeler
Cartographer: Elmari Kuyler
Picture Researcher: Shavonne Johannes
Consultant: Angelia Teo
Proofreader: Claudia dos Santos

Reproduction by Resolution (Cape Town) and
Hirt & Carter (Pty) Ltd, Cape Town
Printed and bound by Times Offset (M) Sdn. Bhd.,
Malaysia.

Although every effort has been made to ensure
that this guide is up to date and current at time
of going to print, the Publisher accepts no
responsibility or liability for any loss, injury or
inconvenience incurred by readers or travellers
using this guide.

Photographic Credits:
Bintan Resort Management Pte Ltd: page 83;
Tom Cockrem: page 72;
Gerald Cubitt: pages 14, 78, 79, 82, 84;
Elle Magazine: page 81;
Jill Gocher: cover, pages 7, 8, 11, 12, 13 (top),
15, 19, 22, 23, 24, 25, 26, 30, 31, 33, 36, 37,
40, 41, 42, 44, 45, 47, 52, 53, 54, 65, 66, 69,
70, 71, 73, 75;
Steve Lovegrove/Picture Tasmania: page 27;
Neil McAllister: pages 6, 34 (top and bottom),
46, 60, 61;
NHIL/Shaen Adey: pages 18, 76;
NHIL/Ryno Reyneke: pages 1, 9, 10, 16, 17,
20, 21, 28, 29, 32, 49, 50, 51;
Radin Mohammed Noh: page 80;
Christine Osborne: pages 13 (bottom), 62;
Travel Ink/Emmanuel Agbaraojo: page 39;
Travel Ink/Nigel Bowen-Morris: page 35;
Travel Ink/Abbie Enock: pages 43, 74;
[NHIL: New Holland Image Library]

Front Cover: *Skyscrapers and traditional shophouses flank the Singapore River.*
Title Page: *The façade of an elegantly restored
shophouse in the heart of Chinatown.*

CONTENTS

USING THIS BOOK

MAKE THE MOST OF YOUR GUIDE

Reading these two pages will help you to get the most out of your guide and save you time when using it. Sites discussed in the text are cross-referenced with the cover maps – for example, the reference 'Map G–C3' refers to the Little India Map (Map G), column C, row 3. Use the Map Plan below to quickly locate the map you need.

MAP PLAN

Outside Back Cover   Outside Front Cover

Inside Front Cover   Inside Back Cover

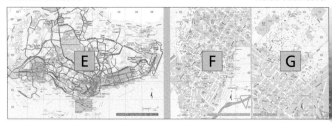

THE BIGGER PICTURE

Key to Map Plan

A – Excursions
B – Jurong
C – Metro Map of Singapore
D – Sentosa
E – Singapore and Surrounds
F – City Centre and
      Chinatown
G – Little India
H – Orchard Road
I – East Coast Area

4

USING THIS BOOK

Key to Symbols

- ⊠ — address
- ☎ — telephone
- ✆ — fax
- 🖥 — website
- 🖱 — e-mail address
- 🕀 — opening times
- 🚌 — transport
- 💰 — entry fee
- 🍽 — restaurants nearby
- **M** — nearest MRT station

Map Legend

motorway	═══════	main road	Orchard
national road	▬▬▬▬▬	other road	Bideford
main road	▬▬▬▬▬	hotel	Ⓗ CHINATOWN
river	Kallang	post office	⊠
city	SINGAPORE	building of interest	Treasury Building
major town	⊙ Johor Bahru	hospital	⊕
national park	Bukit Batok Lake Garden	shopping centre	Chinatown Plaza Ⓢ
airport	✈	tourist information	🛈
MRT line	─ ─ ─ ─	place of worship	△ Church △ Mosque Temple
metro station	● Clarke Quay	one-way street	←
railway	────────	police station	●
peaks in metres	165 m ▲ Bukit Timah	park & garden	Fort Canning Park
place of interest	● Singapore Science Centre	built-up area	
ferry	⛴ ─ ─		
golf course	⚑		

Keep us Current

Travel information is apt to change, which is why we regularly update our guides. We'd be most grateful to receive feedback from you if you've noted something we should include in our updates. If you have any new information, please share it with us by writing to the Publishing Manager, Globetrotter, at the office nearest to you (addresses on the imprint page of this guide). The most significant contribution to each new edition will be rewarded with a free copy of the updated guide.

Above: *Cavenagh Bridge links the colonial core of the city with the business district.*

SINGAPORE

It was Sir Stamford Raffles' dream to trans-form this swamp-covered, pirate-infested island into a 'new Alexandria of the Far East'. His hopes for his new settlement were not misplaced: Singapore has since grown into an important centre for international trade, communications and tourism. It is a great holiday destination with matchless tourist facilities, an excellent transportation system, superb hotels with all the sophistica-tion and comfort of the West, and an enthralling melée of cultures.

It is a country of many contrasts. Hi-tech skyscrapers soar up among picturesque old buildings, and the people still adhere to their ancient traditions, despite living in one of the most advanced countries in the world. The heart and soul of the city is in the ethnic quarters of Chinatown, Arab Street and Little India, but nature lovers will be surprised by the many pockets of green in this bustling city.

For the epicure, Singapore is one big scrumptious feast. In this United Nations of food, styles range from Chinese, Malay and Indian to almost any international cuisine you might wish to try.

Singapore should be included on any traveller's itinerary, whether for pleasure or business. Its attractions lure over six million visitors to the Lion City every year.

The Land

The Republic of Singapore is separated from Peninsular Malaysia by the Straits of Johor and from the Indonesian archipelago in the south by the Straits of Singapore. Its territory consists of the island of Singapore and 58 islets of which more than 20 are inhabited. About 50% of the main island of Singapore is devoted to residential, commercial and industrial development and only some 2% is agricultural land.

Plant Life

Singapore, having evolved from a swampy island clad in tropical rainforest into a thriving city, has lost most of its primary vegetation to urban development. Forests were cut down to make way for agriculture and the expanding population. Today, only a few pockets of primary vegetation remain in protected areas such as the **Bukit Timah Nature Reserve**. Here, the forest consists mainly of the tropical hardwoods of the dipterocarp family (trees with two-winged seeds), some of which grow to a height of 40m (130ft), forming a green canopy over the other vegetation. Non-dipterocarps like *jelutong*, *jambu* and oaks are also found here. Epiphytes – plants which grow on other plants, usually trees – such as the bird's nest fern and the staghorn fern use these forest trees as their hosts.

About 500ha (1250 acres) of **mangrove swamp** prevail along the northern coastline of Kranji and along Sungei Loyang and Sungei Tampines near Pasir Ris. There are patches of marshland in Woodlands and Ulu Pandan and on the northern islands of Pulau Ubin and Pulau Tekong. Along the coast, a variety of grasses, sedges and creepers is found in the sandy areas.

Climate
With its proximity to the equator, Singapore has a tropical climate with a uniformly high average daytime temperature of 31°C (88°F) and a minimum of 23°C (73°F) at night all year. Relative humidity is about 85%, moderated by the prevailing cool sea breeze. Rain falls all year but is heaviest during the northeast monsoon season (Nov–Jan) with an average annual rainfall of 2360mm (93 inches). The driest month is July. February is usually the sunniest month while December has the least sunshine. From Apr–Nov, early morning thunderstorms known as 'Sumatras' occur three or four times a month.

Below: *Singapore's lush vegetation survives in parts of the less developed northern region.*

Hills of Singapore
In the hilly central region of the island, the highest point is Bukit Timah at 165m (542ft), followed by Bukit Gombak (139m; 456ft), Bukit Panjang (132m; 433ft), Bukit Batok (106m; 348ft) and Bukit Mandai (88m; 289ft). Mount Faber, with its view over the harbour, rises to 116m (380ft).

Animal Life

A surprising variety of wildlife is found in this highly urbanized country. In the high canopy of the forest live **vertebrates** such as the flying lemur, two species of squirrel, long-tailed macaques and the flying lizard. The lower canopy is home to shrews, rats, snakes and tree frogs, while lizards, skinks, frogs, snakes and tortoises inhabit the forest floor. The fruit bat, horseshoe bat, tomb bat, the Malayan flying fox and the Malayan false vampire are found here. The tiny mouse-deer, the porcupine and the scaly anteater (or pangolin) survive in Singapore but are rarely seen. Colourful butterflies, moths, beetles and dragonflies abound. A total of 320 **bird species**, including migrants, is currently chronicled.

Aquatic and **insect** life includes tadpoles, prawns, potamonid crabs, water bugs, dragonfly and damselfly nymphs, and fish such as rasbora, puntius, betta, trichogaster and tilapia. Mussels, barnacles, snails, crabs, mud-lobsters, prawns and mudskippers dwell in the mangrove swamps, while the open water is the habitat of glass fish, half-beaks and archer fish. Some tidal **invertebrates** like ghost crabs, bivalves and gastropods are found on the seashore at low tide while high tides bring in the sea slatters.

Singapore's offshore waters, albeit murky, support a rich tropical **marine life**. Corals, gorgonians, anemones, clown fish, feathery tube worms, sinister-looking clusters of black sea-urchins, and the occasional poisonous scorpion fish form the reef colony.

Below: *The park around MacRitchie Reservoir contains areas of primary rainforest and away from the main forest track, popular with joggers, it is rich in wildlife.*

History in Brief
Colonial Singapore: the Days of Raffles

In the 18th century, Britain saw the need to establish a port of call in the east to refresh and protect her merchant fleet, as well as to thwart the Dutch in the East Indies. A trading post had been established in **Penang** by Francis Light in 1786, but **Thomas Stamford Raffles**, then Lieutenant-Governor of Bencoolen in Sumatra, recognized that a more strategically placed settlement was vital. He was given permission to establish such a post and, after surveying nearby islands, landed in Singapore on 29 January 1819.

Raffles saw great potential in the strategically located island. After negotiating a deal with the local rulers, a formal treaty was concluded. The settlement grew rapidly and by 1823, Singapore surpassed Penang in importance. Its free-port status attracted traders from all over Asia and from as far afield as the Middle East and the USA. By 1860 the population, a mere 150 in 1819, had grown to 80,792 and consisted primarily of Chinese, followed by Indians and Malays.

Above: *A tableau depicts the British accepting Japanese surrender in 1945.*

Early History

Singapore seems to have been a small seaport in the period when the mighty Sumatran **Sri Vijaya Empire** ruled the region. According to the 16th-century *Sejarah Melayu*, or 'Malay Annals', **Temasek**, as it was then known, was a flourishing trading post in the 14th century. However, a contemporary Chinese account describes it as a pirate island. It was briefly ruled by the Sumatran prince Parameswara, but invasions by Thais and Javanese in the 1390s drove him to flee north to Melaka to found the Malay Sultanate there. **Singa Pura** remained undeveloped until the arrival of Raffles.

Above: *Kranji Memorial and Cemetery, in memory of those who perished in the Pacific War.*

The Fall of Singapore
The peace and prosperity of the city was shattered in the early hours of 8 December 1941 when it was bombed by Japanese aircraft. Singapore, which had been considered an impregnable fortress by the British, was occupied by the Japanese on 15 February 1942 and renamed **Syonan** ('Light of the South'). The occupation lasted for three and a half years, during which time great oppression was inflicted on the people and many lives were lost.

Modern History
After the Japanese surrender in 1945, Singapore came under British Military Administration until March 1946, when the Straits Settlements (Penang, Melaka and Singapore) were dissolved. Singapore became a Crown Colony, and Penang and Melaka joined the Malayan Union. The country attained self-government in 1959 and the first general election was held to elect 51 representatives to the Legislative Assembly. The People's Action Party (PAP) won a majority of 43 seats and **Lee Kuan Yew** became the first prime minister of Singapore. The PAP joined with the communists to fight British colonialism, but conflicts of ideology between the two factions led to a split in 1961. In that year Singapore joined Malaya, and on 16 September 1963 was included in the merger between the Federation of Malaya, Sarawak and North Borneo (now Sabah) to form **Malaysia**. But on 9 August 1965 Singapore left Malaysia to become a sovereign, democratic and independent nation, and on 22 December of that year it became a republic.

The 1970s saw political stability and a high rate of economic growth led by the PAP which emerged triumphant from the 1968 general election, setting a pattern for all subsequent elections and holding every seat until 1981. After 31 years in office, Lee Kuan Yew stepped down in 1990 and Goh Chok Tong became the second prime minister of Singapore – one of the great success stories of Asia.

Government and Economy

Singapore is a republic with a parliamentary system of government based on universal adult suffrage. Voting is compulsory for all citizens over 21. The head of state is the **president** (elected by the people every six years) who selects his cabinet on the advice of the **prime minister**. The administration of the government devolves upon the cabinet headed by the prime minister, who is appointed by the president.

The unicameral **parliament** consists of 83 members elected by secret ballot, and serves a minimum of five years. The People's Action Party (PAP) has been in power since 1959, when Lee Kuan Yew became the country's first prime minister.

Singapore's **legal system** is based on the British judiciary system. The Supreme Court is presided over by the chief justice and other judges appointed by the president. The Shariah is a religious court framed by Islamic law with jurisdiction over domestic disputes between Muslims.

Singapore's advantageous geographical position contributes to its importance as a world centre for **commerce** and **industry**. Manufacturing, finance and business services are the greatest contributors to its GDP. Despite rapid economic growth, inflation has remained low.

The **manufacturing** sector concentrates on electronic products and components, while machinery, industrial chemicals, paints, pharmaceuticals, food, printing and publishing are also big.

Finance and Investment
Singapore has a key position as an international financial and banking centre, notably for the Asia-Pacific region. It has continued to attract considerable **foreign investment**. To lure more foreign investors, there are attractive incentives such as tax concessions and unrestricted repatriation or importation of capital, profits, dividends and royalties. Blessed with a perceptive government, an educated and industrious population and a competent constitution, Singapore has blazed a trail towards its desired status as a developed country.

Below: *The classical façade of the Supreme Court, an imposing monument of the colonial era, completed in 1939.*

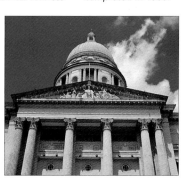

One Kind Language, Catch No Ball!

Singapore's unique vernacular, called **Singlish**, is a mixture of English and local dialects:

Lah • Used at the end of a sentence to add emphasis.

One kind • Describes a type of place or person: 'He is one kind lah.'

Go fly kite • Get lost.

Catch no ball • Cannot understand.

Kiasu • Afraid to lose out (Singaporeans hate missing out on things, especially if they have paid for them).

Can or not? • Asking a favour: 'Go with me, can or not?'

Ang mo • Any Caucasian.

Kay poh • A busybody or chatterbox.

Alamak • Expression of shock or surprise.

Aiyah • Exasperation or frustration: 'Aiyah, so hot one!'

Wah • Incredibility: 'Wah! she is so pretty.'

Go-stan • To go astern or reverse (as in a car).

The People

Migrants and merchants from China, India, Indonesia, the Malay Peninsula and the Middle East came in search of a better place to settle down, lured by the riches of the land and bringing with them their own cultures, languages, customs and festivals. Through intermarriage and integration, these diverse human 'ingredients' have merged into the multi-faceted society that is unique to Singapore today: a young nation with a vibrant and diverse cultural heritage.

The Chinese

Of Singapore's 150 inhabitants in 1819, 30 were Chinese farmers engaged in pepper and gambier cultivation. But the new trading opportunities soon began to attract a continuous stream of Chinese immigrants. By the mid-19th century, Chinese immigration was well organized. Most arrived as indentured labourers. Having incurred heavy debts to pay for their passage, they were inevitably exploited as forced labour by their sponsors, until the indenture system was abolished in 1914.

By 1912 the Chinese population had risen to 250,000 in number. The motives of the Chinese for leaving their poverty-stricken and war-torn homeland were purely economic, and they continued to pledge their loyalty to their motherland. Today the Chinese form the largest ethnic group of Singapore's population, and the economy of the country is their stronghold. They fervently preserve their traditions and customs and Chinatown still bears witness to the various colourful and ancient festivals the Chinese brought with them.

The Indians

Indians began to arrive in Singapore as soon as the island was established as a British trading post. The promise of ample employment drew Indians from Penang, India and Sri Lanka seeking work as civil servants, teachers, technicians and traders. When the

British decided to make Singapore a penal station in 1823, several hundred Indian prisoners were brought in as convict labourers to build government offices and other parts of the colony's infrastructure. Indians continued to flood in until immigration controls were imposed in the early 1950s.

Although almost all major Indian ethnic groups are represented in Singapore, about 80% are from southern India. They maintain a strong bond with their native land by preserving their religion, customs and festivals. Little India is 'a home from home' for the Indian community.

*Ancient traditions still abound in ultramodern Singaporean society: citrus plants flank an entrance to ward off evil spirits (**above**) and fortune tellers thrive (**below**). **Opposite:** One of the many faces of Singapore: about 7% of the population is of Indian extraction.*

The Islamic Community

The prospect of a more prosperous life drew Singapore's neighbours to its shores as early immigrants. From the Malay Peninsula came the Malays, from Indonesia, the Sumatrans, Javanese, Bugis and the Balinese. Despite regional differences in cultures and dialects, the Muslim community, including the Arabs who mainly arrived later as merchants, integrated well. Their traditional cultures and customs are still evident today in the Islamic quarter in Arab Street.

Night Safari
✉ 80 Mandai Lake Road
☎ (65) 6269 3411
🖳 www.
nightsafari.com.sg
🕐 19:30–00:00 daily
💰 SGD15.75 (adult)
SGD10.50 (child)
🚌 Buses SBS138, 171, Tibs927
Ⓜ Ang Mo Kio or Yio Chu Kang

Jurong Bird Park
✉ 2 Jurong Hill
☎ (65) 6265 0022
🖳 www.
birdpark.com.sg
🕐 09:00–17:00 daily
💰 SGD12.25 (adult)
SGD5.10 (child)
🚌 Buses SBS194, 251
Ⓜ Boon Lay

Opposite: *The 'Panorail' takes visitors around Jurong Bird Park, to see this spectacular avian collection in its beautiful setting.*
Below: *Malaysian tigers are a protected species.*

✪ *See* Map E–D2   ★ ★ ★

NIGHT SAFARI

The world's first and only Night Safari Park was opened in May 1994. Adjacent to the Zoo, the 40ha (100-acre) park is laid out in a natural setting of tropical rainforest on a hillside. Trees cleared during construction were replanted to preserve the environment. There are 1000 nocturnal creatures of about 100 different species living in spacious natural habitats under subtle moonglow lighting. A 45-minute tram journey with running commentary covers the highlights of the zoo, guiding you round geographical regions: a Nepalese river valley, Equatorial Africa, the South American pampas, Asian riverine forest or a Burmese hillside.

Clearly marked trails are named after various animals, and following these you weave through the forest along the dimly lit paths. The animals are bathed in special lighting which does not disturb their nocturnal habits. The atmosphere is thrilling: the incessant song of the cicadas is punctuated by the calls of animals great and small in a captivating natural symphony. The indigenous animals of each region, kept safe without obvious barriers, carry on their nightly routines oblivious of the spectators.

In order not to alarm the animals, silence should be observed and no flash photography is allowed, as constant exposure to the lights could blind the nocturnal creatures.

See Map B–A3 | ★★★

JURONG BIRD PARK

This park claims to contain the world's largest, most impressive aviaries, covering an area of 20ha (50 acres). It is home to 7000 birds of 600 species, kept in huge enclosures.

Before starting out, it is advisable to take an orientation trip on the **Panorail**, the air-conditioned monorail system which affords an overview of the park with a running commentary on the main attractions.

Using the park's map, a walking tour is a highly recommended way to appreciate properly the wonderful collections of the feathered kind. Don't miss the bird show in the **Pools Amphitheatre**, with its colourful macaws, owls, eagles and condors, and the **Penguin Parade** enclosure in a carefully air-conditioned Antarctic setting with some 200 penguins of five species as well as 50 seabirds. The **Walk-in Aviary** is a must with its 2ha (5-acre) netted enclosure, complete with a man-made waterfall and 100 species of free-flying tropical birds in a naturalistic habitat. The park claims to have the biggest collections of hornbills and South American toucans in the world. There is a simulated tropical thunderstorm daily at midday.

If you are an 'early bird' you can have your breakfast on the **Songbird Terrace** to the accompaniment of the singing birds. Check the commencement of bird shows and feeding times locally.

See Map F–D3	★ ★ ★

ASIAN CIVILISATIONS MUSEUM

Located on two sites (one in Empress Place and the other on Armenian Street) the ACM exhibits archaeological treasures from China and other ancient Asian civilizations.

Asian Civilisations Museum

✉ 1 Empress Place
☎ (65) 6332 7798
🖳 www.nhb.gov.sg/ACM/acm.shtml
🕑 Mon 13:00–19:00, Tue–Sun 09:00–19:00, Fri 09:00–21:00, free entry after 19:00
🚌 SBS 10, 70, 82, 97, 100, 107, 130,162, 196, Tibs 167, 700
Ⓜ Raffles Place
💰 adults SG$5.00, students & pensioners SG$2.50, children under 6 free

✉ 39 Armenian Street
🖳 www.museum.org.sg/ACM/acm.shtml
🕑 same opening hours as for Empress Place
🚌 SBS 7, 14. 16, 36, 97, 131, 162, Tibs 77, 167, 171, 700
Ⓜ City Hall
💰 adults SG$3.00, students & pensioners SG$1.50, children under 6 free

Empress Place

Spread over three levels, the newly restored neo-Classical Empress Place Museum houses 11 galleries with over 1300 artefacts charting the civilizations of China, Southeast Asia, South Asia and West Asia/Islam. The exhibits are innovatively displayed and well documented; the themed galleries have multimedia and interactive components. Talking heads featuring the nationalities of Singapore, with touch-sensor television screens, are sited in each section to guide visitors through the exhibits. Don't miss the Singapore River Interpretive Gallery which tells the moving story of immigrants who lived and worked on the Singapore River. There are special exhibitions which change every three to four months throughout the year. The library has a collection of 11,000 books, journals and catalogues and rare books dating back to the 1850s. ACM Empress Place also has a museum shop, a fully equipped auditorium and a function room with a spectacular view of the Singapore River.

ASIAN CIVILISATIONS MUSEUM

See Map F–C1   ★ ★ ★

Armenian Street (Peranakan Museum)

Located at the former Tao Nan School, it was first opened in April 1997, to showcase mostly Chinese civilization. Today, most of its galleries are devoted to the Peranakan (meaning 'born here' in Malay) culture. The Peranakans are the descendants of Chinese who intermarried the local people, integrating with the Malays, Indians and Eurasians. They are renowned for their intricate beadworks on shoes; fine embroidery on their female costumes called *kebaya*; porcelain, silverware and jewellery, which are all on display in different categories in the galleries. Their Nyonya cuisine is renowned in Singapore and Malaysia. It is an epicurean marriage of Chinese cooking methods with Malay and Indian spices and a touch of innovative adaptation from the three cultures. The museum charts the origin and history of this unique mixed race – their crossed culture of Chinese with Malay forms one of the most unique races in Southeast Asia. The exhibits are painstakingly researched to bring to life the fascinating and eclectic Peranakan culture. There are plans to develop this museum into a full-fledged Peranakan-themed museum in the next 3 to 5 years due to the Peranakans' importance in the Singapore society. The continuous special exhibitions change every three to four months throughout the year.

> ### The Peranakans
> It is believed the origins of the Peranakans date back to the 15th century when Sultan Mansur Shah of the Malacca Sultanate married the Chinese princess Hang Lih Po during the Ming dynasty. She brought with her a noble retinue of 500. From their liaisons with the local Malays were born the Peranakans who are known as Babas (male) and Nyonyas (female). In addition many Chinese merchants settled in the Straits which comprised Singapore, Malacca and Penang, and married the local women (hence the Peranakans are known as 'Straits Chinese').

*The ACM at Empress Place (**opposite**) and at Armenian Street (**below**).*

See Map F–B2/C3 ★ ★ ★

CIVIC DISTRICT AND SINGAPORE RIVER

Opposite Raffles Landing Site on the southern bank of the Singapore River is the **Boat Quay Conservation Area**. The once busy cargo loading bays have been transformed into a tourist attraction. Shophouses, warehouses and godowns have been spruced up and converted into restaurants, bars and entertainment centres. Bumboats which once carried cargo now transport tourists on river cruises. Join one of these (best at high tide) for views of riverside Singapore set against the gleaming skyscrapers.

Clarke Quay is also an area of restored warehouses and shophouses. It is clustered with market stalls set up on push carts, a choice of restaurants, bars and open-air eating places. Clowns on stilts and wayside portrait artists entertain the passers-by.

Clarke Quay is divided into five areas: Merchants' Court, the Cannery, Shophouse Row, Traders' Market and the Foundry. Clarke Quay is also home to the biggest Sunday flea market in Singapore. There are more than 120 market stalls and makeshift tables, where the vendors sell anything from antique porcelain to that rare 1977 'Han Solo' Star Wars toy figurine. The cannery block is where toy aficionados gather to hawk high-value dolls, playthings and sometimes vintage clocks, watches and posters.

Bumboat Trips
Don't miss seeing the city from the deck of a boat. A bumboat trip along the Singapore River offers a nostalgic reminder of the days when these wooden boats carried cargo, not tourists. Old godowns and shophouses which have been restored and transformed into shops and restaurants (notably at Clarke Quay and Boat Quay) set the scene on the waterfront. The trips pass landmarks such as Raffles Landing Site, Parliament House and the Merlion Statue. River cruises depart from Parliament Steps, Clifford Pier and Liang Court.

Below: *In the Boat Quay Conservation Area the river bank, once crowded with cargo boats and hawker stalls, is now lined with tables set out in front of the bars and restaurants housed in the converted shophouses.*

⭐ *See* Map F–B4   ★ ★ ★

CHINATOWN

The kaleidoscopic feast of colour is the first thing that will dazzle visitors to Chinatown. The rainbow hues of all manner of goods, clustered in the shops and spilling over into the five-foot way, are mesmerizing. The pungent smell of traditional Chinese medicine will assault your nostrils at the same time as the tantalizing aromas from the coffee shops. Watch out for the famous sweet barbecued pork being grilled over red-hot charcoal along the five-foot way.

Stroll through Club Street and Ann Siang Road, and you will see songbirds tweeting away in their gilded cages while the 'informal national flag of Singapore' – washing draped over long bamboo poles – flutters in the soft breeze. A discreet peer into a shophouse through old-fashioned wooden bars across the door will reveal ancestral altars.

Many craftsmen ply their age-old trades in these crowded streets. There is the clog maker, knocking into shape the traditional wooden footwear. For the tea connoisseur there are quaint little tea shops that raise tea-making into an art form and offer a vast choice of tea and utensils. The ancient art of calligraphy is still evident, while effigy and joss-stick makers are kept busy by the continuing demand for traditional Chinese funeral rites. Shops in Temple Street and Sago Street make cane and coloured paper effigies of houses, cars, money and other necessaries, which are burnt to journey with the deceased into the next world.

Above: *A fortune teller with her attendant parrot.*

Fortune-telling

In spite of their modern image, Singaporeans still seek the advice of fortune-tellers to guide them in their future. A businessman would not build an office block or a house without first consulting the feng shui expert, the geomancer, to find a favourable site and auspicious position for the building. Women can be seen at temples casting kidney-shaped wooden blocks, called *mu bei*, to the ground: the way the blocks fall shows an answer from the gods. Advice can also be had by shaking bamboo fortune-telling sticks from a container until one falls out. The inscriptions on the sticks are interpreted by a temple attendant. Along Serangoon Road, fortunes are told from cards picked by parrots, from which the fortune-teller will spin a tale of your future.

☼ *See* Map F–B4 | ★ ★ ★

CHINATOWN HERITAGE CENTRE

Located in the heart of Chinatown at Pagoda Street in three restored shophouses, the centre charts the history and traditions of the early Chinese immigrants. The atmospheric exhibits – aided by sights, sounds and smells – are housed

Above: *Chinatown Heritage Centre.*

in three levels with each level recreating an aspect of the immigrants' lifestyle, rituals and tribulations. On the ground floor, a traditional retail shop and a typical Chinese coffee shop known locally as *Kopitiam* are faithfully recreated, while the second floor, using clever lighting, sets an atmosphere of gloom as it shows immigrants embarking on the long perilous journey to Singapore to escape poverty and war in China and seek a better future in Southeast Asia. It also illustrates the darker side of the community indulging in the 'Four Sins' – opium, prostitutes, gambling and secret societies.

On the third level, the ambience is lifted with the more positive aspects of the immigrants' lives during the 1950s – the golden era of Chinatown – with lively street markets, festivals and religious celebrations. It touches on the funeral rites and rituals, focussing on the history of Sago Lane, renowned at one time for its 'death houses' for the terminally ill and for making paper effigies of luxury goods to be burnt at funerals for the benefit of the dead.

Chinatown Heritage Centre
✉ 48 Pagoda Street
☎ (65) 6325 2872
📠 (65) 6325 2879
🖳 www.chinatown heritage.com.sg
🕘 10:00–19:00 Mon–Thu, 10:00–22:00 Fri–Sun
💰 adults SG$8.00, children SG$4.80
Ⓜ Chinatown

🌀 *See* Map D–A1   ★ ★ ★

UNDERWATER WORLD, SENTOSA

Asia's largest tropical oceanarium houses over 2000 species of fish kept in a series of aquaria including a giant acrylic funnel rising from the floor in which visitors can view the fish from all angles. The highlight is the 90m (100yd) submerged acrylic tunnel which allows you to travel under the water on a moving walkway to view the marine life. It is a fantastic aquatic experience to be surrounded by menacing sharks, leered at by moray eels lurking in the rocks and swept over by sting-rays without even getting wet. Divers sometimes swim among the fish offering them morsels of food. A marine theatre projects a continuous educational film on the conservation of sea life.

A new addition is the **Dolphin Lagoon** at Central Beach. Built at a cost of SG$3 million, its latest attraction is the Indo-Pacific humpbacked dolphin, more commonly known as the pink dolphin. The lagoon is built to simulate the natural habitat of the dolphins in the wild. Visitors can watch the dolphin show or swim with the dolphins.

Underwater World
✉ 85 Siloso Road, Sentosa
☎ (65) 6275 0030
📱 (65) 6275 0036
📧 uwspl@underwater world.com.sg
🖥 www.underwaterworld.com
🕑 09:00–21:00 daily (Night Ocean opens from 19:00 onwards)
👤 adults SG$17.30, children 3–12 years SG$11.20 (including admission to Dolphin Lagoon); swim with dolphins SG$85.00
🚌 Sentosa Bus from World Trade Centre Bus Terminal; on Sentosa take bus on Blue, Green and Red Line. Monorail – alight at M2
Ⓜ Tiong Bahru

Below: *The moving walkway below the water at Underwater World.*

See Map E–E4

★ ★ ★

Singapore Botanic Gardens
✉ Holland Road
☎ (65) 6471 9933
🖥 www.nparks.gov.sg
🕐 05:00–00:00 daily
(National Orchid Garden
open 08:30–19:00)
⏣ Botanic Gardens
free, National Orchid
Garden SG$2 (adult),
SG$1.00 (students and
senior citizens), free
(children under 12)
🚌 SBS 7, 77, 123,
174, 105, 106. Tibs 75
M Orchard

Below: *Singapore Botanic Gardens, a tranquil respite from the city heat.*

SINGAPORE BOTANIC GARDENS

Close to the city, not far from the top end of Orchard Road, the Botanic Gardens were founded in 1859, and now provide a green refuge for those wanting to escape from the suffocating city atmosphere. Covering an area of 52ha (130 acres), vistas of rolling green lawns are punctuated with bursts of colour from a profusion of orchids and other flowering plants. The gardens' orchidarium displays 250 orchid species and hybrids. In contrast, the landscape includes the green canopy of primary forest with their huge diversity of plant species. The landscape is further enhanced by the lakes, inhabited by carp, waterfowl and kingfishers. Outdoor concerts are regularly held here, while newly-weds frequently make a beeline for the most scenic spot in the gardens for photo shoots.

In 1877, these gardens saw the origin of the Malayan rubber industry when Henry Ridley planted eleven Brazilian rubber tree seedlings propagated in London's Kew Gardens. There is a memorial to Ridley, who was director of the gardens from 1888 to 1912, on the spot where the original trees were planted.

See Map E–D2 ★★

SINGAPORE ZOOLOGICAL GARDENS

Singapore Zoo, with an enviable collection of animals, is one of the finest and most beautiful in the world. Its breeding programmes and educational shows are the pride of the zoo.

Catch **breakfast with the orang-utans**, to meet the matriarch of the group, Ah Meng. A primate expert gives a talk on one of our closest relatives and the need to protect this endangered species, while the apes themselves listen attentively.

Above: *The world's heaviest lizard, the Komodo dragon.*

Other attractions include the **lions'** glass viewing gallery, where you are only a purr away from the king of the beasts. You can 'rub noses' with the mighty **polar bears** in their underwater tank, or see the **sealions** and **penguins** frolicking in their simulated Antarctic habitat. Here you will also find the **Komodo dragons** from Indonesia, the only ones outside their native land.

Next door to the zoo is **Mandai Orchid Gardens**, an orchid-covered hill which is the country's largest commercial garden, established in 1950. A colourful display of orchids can be admired throughout the year. The water gardens blanketed with water-lilies complete the effect of floral profusion. Visitors can purchase gift-wrapped orchids; convention groups can have new orchid hybrids named after them to commemorate their visit.

<u>Singapore Zoological Gardens</u>
✉ 80 Mandai Lake Rd
☎ (65) 6269 3411
✆ info@zoo.com.sg
🖳 www.zoo.com.sg
🕑 08:30–18:00 daily
🚌 SBS 138, 171. Tibs 927
M Ang Mo Kio or Yio Chu Kang
💰 adults SG$14.00, children SG$7

<u>Mandai Orchid Gardens</u>
✉ Mandai Lake Road
☎ (65) 6793 5480
📠 (65) 6793 5482
✆ mandaigarden@singaporeorchids.com.sg
🖳 www.mandai.com.sg
🚌 SBS 138, 171. Tibs 927
M Ang Mo Kio or Yio Chu Kang
🕑 09:00–17:00 daily
💰 adults SG$3, children under 12 SG$1

☼ *See* Map F–D3   ★ ★

RAFFLES LANDING SITE AND ARTS HOUSE

Raffles Landing Site on North Boat Quay is marked by a white marble replica of the statue of Singapore's founder, standing guard over a widened stretch of the Singapore River known as 'the belly of the carp'. There are several historical buildings and interesting landmarks in this area, including the Empress Place branch of the **Asian Civilisations Museum** (*see* page 16) and the **Victoria Theatre** (*see* page 72).

Formerly known as the Old Parliament House, **Arts House** was designed and built by the Irish architect George Coleman in 1826 as a Neo-Palladian mansion for John Argyle Maxwell, a Scottish merchant who leased it out to the government for use as a courthouse. Throughout the years, it also served as the Assembly House and the Parliament House. Today, it is a venue for the arts and the only historic building refurbished with modern amenities. Its aim is to provide a platform for Asian designers to showcase their work and to facilitate a lively and varied calendar of events for the performing arts. Its 3000m² (32,280 sq ft) of space is designated for theatre and dance productions, musical performances and fashion shows. The former library is a visual art space while the old administration office is now a 75-seat cinema. There are three food and beverage outlets, and a studio for yoga and dance classes.

Arts House
✉ 1 Old Parliament Lane, Level 2 Annex Building
☎ (65) 6332 6900
📠 (65) 6339 9695
✉ enquiries@toph.com.sg
🖥 www.theartshouse.com.sg
🕐 10:00–20:00 Mon–Fri, 11:00–20:00 Sat–Sun
🚌 32, 51, 61, 63, 80, 103, 124, 145, 166, 174, 195, 197, 603, 851, 961
M Raffles Place and Clarke Quay
💰 Admission free; guided tours (45 mins long, from 11:00–15:00) including short film and a drink SG\$8.00

See Map G	★★

LITTLE INDIA

In essence, the district around Serangoon Road is the Indian sub-continent condensed and transported to Singapore. Originally a swamp, the siting of brick kilns and lime-pits here by the colonial government in the 1820s led Indian labourers to settle in the district, and they made it their own.

Little India features all aspects of Indian culture and customs, including several Hindu temples (*see* page 35). The aroma of spices and jasmine hangs in the air of the narrow streets, flanked by shophouses selling garlands of flowers strung by men with nimble fingers to decorate altars, adorn a woman's hair or a taxi driver's dashboard shrine. Some shops stock special Indian cosmetics: turmeric powder or cream for the complexion, henna to decorate the hands and feet, especially for weddings, perfumed oils for the skin and kohl pencils for the eyes. Others specialize in spices for Indian cuisine and there are communal mills to which housewives bring their fresh spice mixtures each day to be ground by the miller for a small fee. The tempting aroma of curry wafts from numerous restaurants and stalls sell colourful Indian sweetmeats.

The **Tekka Centre** in Buffalo Road is an interesting place to explore, with its large wet market, food centres and shops selling electronic equipment, clothes and bric-à-brac at bargain prices.

Little India's Street Names
Many of the area's streets bear the names of colonial politicians or army personnel who served in India. Hastings Road is named after Warren Hastings, the first governor-general of Bengal; Clive Street after Robert Clive, Baron of Plassey, who consolidated British control of India in 1757; and Campbell Lane after Sir Colin Campbell who suppressed the Indian mutiny and freed Lucknow in 1857.

Opposite: *This white marble statue of Thomas Stamford Raffles, the city's visionary founder, seems to gaze over the Singapore River.*
Below: *A vivid piece of carving at the Sri Veeramakaliamman Temple.*

Changi Prison Chapel and Museum
✉ 1000 Upper Changi Road North
☎ (65) 6214 2451
📠 (65) 6214 1179
📧 changi_museum@pacific.net.sg
🖥 www.changimuseum.com
🚌 SBS 2, 29
Ⓜ Tanah Merah and Tampines
🕘 09:30–17:00 daily
♿ Admission free

🌸 *See* Map E–I3   ★★

CHANGI PRISON CHAPEL AND MUSEUM

The open-air Changi Prison Chapel is a simple wooden affair with a thatched roof over the altar. It is a replica, constructed by inmates of the prison, of the original chapel built by Allied prisoners of war in World War II. In the face of adversity and the hopelessness of their situation, the chapel became the focal point of the prisoners' lives as they turned to religion to sustain their spirits. To the right of the outdoor pews is a large notice which encourages visitors to pick flowers from the hibiscus and other flowering shrubs by the chapel and to place them on the altar to honour those who died. On the left wall of the chapel is a notice board where visitors who lost friends or relatives in the war can pin little cards with moving messages of remembrance for their dear departed.

Below: *Changi Prison Chapel, a replica of the simple thatched wooden structure erected by Allied prisoners during World War II.*

Adjacent to the prison chapel is the museum, in which vivid accounts of many of the harrowing experiences of the prisoners of war are illustrated with photographs and paintings. It is an emotional experience to walk round the museum imagining the inhumanity and degradation these prisoners suffered at the hands of the Japanese during the occupation. Changi Prison, which was built to house 600 prisoners, was used to intern 3500 civilian men, women and children after the Allied surrender.

CHANGI CHAPEL & PULAU UBIN

See Map E–H/I2   ★★

PULAU UBIN

Above: *Pulau Ubin represents the rural side of Singapore.*

This small island lying 2km (1.3 miles) off the northeastern coast and measuring 7km (4 miles) in length and 2km (1.3 miles) in width, is like a snapshot of rural Singapore 30 years ago. Malay villages raised on stilts and elevated fish traps called *kelong* make up the rustic scene by the seafront, while orchards, duck, fish and prawn farms are found inland. A hired bicycle is an ideal way to explore, weaving along the many dirt tracks criss-crossing the whole island. Places of interest include Chinese temples (including a cave temple accessible only at low tide from the beach), a Buddhist meditation centre, and a mosque. A lake formed from a disued quarry serves as a swimming pool for weary hikers. Ubin Seafood, the restaurant on this island, is credited with the best seafood cuisine in Singapore.

Ubin Seafood
⊠ 42 Pulau Ubin, Singapore 1750
☎ (65) 6543 2489
🖰 ubinseafood@ yahoo.com.sg
M Tanah Merah (EW4), then take SBS bus 2 or 29 to Changi Village bus interchange, followed by a 10-minute boat ride from the Changi Point jetty.
🝙 The boat ride costs SG$2.00.
🕘 Boats operate from 06:00–23:00.

⊙ *See* Map D–A1   ★★

FORT SILOSO, SENTOSA

Situated at the western tip of the island, this 19th-century British fort was the last bastion of the British forces during the Japanese invasion of Singapore in 1942. It is a maze of look-out points, giant cannons and underground tunnels filled with the re-created sounds of battle. Wax tableaux in the barrack-rooms depict a typical officer's quarters, complete with a nodding greyhound and photographs of the soldier's loved ones; the fort's laundry-room is staffed by a Chinaman, while a Chinese tailor measures an officer for his new uniform. As a bonus, all these scenes are animated, complete with atmospheric sound effects and snippets of conversation. An air-conditioned mini-theatre shows a short film about the war at frequent intervals.

Visitors can stroll among historical figures such as Britain's General Percival, Japan's Lt. General Yamashita and their wax figurine officers from the Surrender Chambers. It is worthwhile browsing through 245 photographs, documents and film clips on display to step back into this chapter of history and gain an insight into the lives of the British forces defending the fort. Check out two new docudramas about the war years, three new routes and some brand new exhibits.

Above: *A recreated wartime scene at Fort Siloso.*
Opposite: *Esplanade-Theatres on the Bay, Singapore's fine cultural centre.*

Fort Siloso
✉ 33 Allanbrooke Road, Sentosa
☎ (65) 6275 0388
🖥 www.sentosa.com.sg
🕐 10:00–18:00 daily
🚆 Sentosa Bus from World Trade Centre Bus Terminal. On Sentosa, take monorail to station M2 or bus on Red, Blue or Green Line and transfer to Fort Train
M Tiong Bahru
💰 adults SG$8, children 3–12 years SG$5

See Map F–E2   ★★

ESPLANADE-THEATRES ON THE BAY

You wouldn't be able to miss the magnificent **Esplanade-Theatres On The Bay** even if you tried. Easily recognizable by its two dome-shaped structures that resemble the local king of fruits, the durian, Esplanade is Singapore's answer to an art hub. Hailed as an architectural marvel, Esplanade has two venues – the theatre and the concert hall – both of which are considered world-class performance venues. Art lovers will find a multitude of treats including symphonic and choral music, both Asian and Western theatre, opera, musicals, dance performances and popular music concerts.

The user-friendly building has facilities for wheelchairs and toilets for the disabled. Tickets for guided tours are available from the Information Centre next to the concert hall foyer. The Esplanade Malls has an array of retail shops and restaurants.

Esplanade-Theatres on the Bay
⊠ 1 Esplanade Drive
☎ (65) 6828 8222
🖳 www.esplanade.com
🚌 SBS 36, 57, 75, 77, 97, 106, 111, 133, 162, 171, 195, 700A, 857, 960/1
M City Hall
🕐 10:00–22:00 (or half an hour after the last performance); for performance times, check with the theatre; guided tours (45 mins long) are available Mon–Fri 11:00–14:00, weekends and public holidays at 11:00.
♿ Admission to the publics spaces is free; guided tours cost SG$8.00 for adults, SG$5 for children 12 years and under.
🍴 Food and drinks are served at the plethora of cafés, bars and restaurants throughout the building.

See Map E–E3/F4

★★

Kong Meng San Phor Kark See Temple
✉ 88 Bright Hill Road
☎ (65) 6453 4046
🖳 www.kmspks.org
M Bishan, and then you can take a taxi to the temple.
♿ Admission free

Siong Lim Temple
✉ 184E Jalan Toa Payoh
☎ (65) 6259 6924
📠 (65) 6353 8147
M Toa Payoh
♿ Admission free

KONG MENG SAN PHOR KARK SEE TEMPLE & SIONG LIM TEMPLE

Reputed to be the largest religious building in Singapore, the Buddhist **Kong Meng San Phor Kark See Temple** in the centre of the island is grandiose not just in size but in its lavish decoration and architectural design. The complex spreads over 8ha (19 acres) and includes shrines, pagodas, pavilions, bridges and a crematorium, all weighed down with mythological figures of dragons, phoenix, figurines and flowers. A large pond in the garden brims with turtles which are released into it by devotees on special occasions to bring good luck.

Located in central Singapore, the extraordinary Buddhist **Siong Lim Temple** (Lian Shan Shuang Lin) was built in 1908 and is now gazetted as a national monument. It was founded by a Chinese abbot to commemorate the birth and death of Buddha, a dedication which gives rise to its name of 'Twin Groves of the Lotus Mountain'. An ornately decorated gateway that is reached across a bridge opens into a courtyard.

Below: *The ornate main hall of the Siong Lim Temple at Toa Payoh.*

The grand building is guarded against evil by the Four Kings of Heaven. There are several shrines dedicated to various deities, including the Goddess of Mercy and the Laughing Buddha: the latter's stomach is often rubbed by visitors who believe the gesture will bring them good luck.

SRI MARIAMMAN TEMPLE

Religious Tolerance
As a strictly secular state, Singapore is anxious to preserve its ethnic harmony by avoiding any hint of fundamentalism or the mixing of religion with politics. The Maintenance of Religious Harmony Act, introduced in 1988, banned attempts by adherents of any one faith to convert others, and barred the teaching of religion in schools.

Left: *A young devotee at the Sri Mariamman Temple, Singapore's oldest and largest Hindu temple.*

Along South Bridge Road is the oldest and largest Hindu temple in the country, built in 1843. It replaced an earlier structure on this same site that was erected in 1827 by Narian Pillai, who had arrived in Singapore on Raffles' own ship.

The magnificent pagoda-like entrance-tower, or *gopuram*, which was restored in 1984, is bedecked with carvings of numerous deities from the Hindu pantheon. Bells and banana fronds frame its doorway, and colourful frescoes span the ceiling. The annual fire-walking festival of **Thimithi** is celebrated at this temple around November, when devotees walk barefoot across a bed of red-hot embers.

Sri Mariamman Temple
✉ 244 South Bridge Road
☎ (65) 6223 4064
🚌 SBS 103, 166, 197 or SMRT Bus 61 from North Bridge Road
M City Hall
♿ Admission Free

See **Map F–B1** | ★

Above: *Fort Canning Park, where the British military had their headquarters.*

THE BATTLE BOX, FORT CANNING

As you stroll up Canning Rise from the Armenian Church, a flight of stairs will lead you to Fort Canning Park, where you will find memorials of the early colonial pioneers and ancient royal Malay tombs. Here lies the **Keramat Iskandar Shah**, believed to be the tomb of the Sumatran prince who became the last king of Temasek, the old name for Singapore, in the 14th century. Thomas Stamford Raffles built his first home here and it was generally believed that this sacred hill of the Malays had brought him the degree of success he enjoyed.

The fort itself, now in ruins, was built in 1859 to protect Singapore and to monitor shipping movement in the harbour. Burrowing through the hillside are the underground **bunkers** which housed the command post of the Allied forces during World War II. One of these, **The Battle Box**, marks the place where General Percival made the decision to surrender to the Japanese; it now houses a re-creation of the occupation through robotic figures and virtual reality viewing of actual footage of the events leading up to the surrender. A 1km trail called the **19th-Century Walk of History** enables visitors to retrace part of the history of that era.

The Battle Box
✉ 51 Canning Rise
☎ (65) 6333 0510
📠 (65) 6333 0590
🕐 10:00–18:00 daily
Ⓜ Dhoby Ghaut
👤 Adults SG\$8.00, children SG\$5.00

☉ *See* Map F–E1 | ★

RAFFLES HOTEL

Affectionately known as 'The Grand Old Lady of the East', Raffles Hotel is redolent of old grandeur, timeless elegance and the celebrities who have been its guests. Founded in 1887, it started out as a humble 10-room hotel located in an old bungalow located at the corner of Beach and Bras Basah roads. More wings were added to the hotel over the next few years and Raffles' familiar main building, in elegant Renaissance style, dates from 1899, when it was the first building in Singapore to be equipped with electric light and the last word in opulence.

Among the many famous people who patronized and immortalized this elegant hotel were Joseph Conrad, Rudyard Kipling, Somerset Maugham, Charlie Chaplin, Maurice Chevalier and Noel Coward.

Raffles Hotel was declared a national monument in 1987, then it closed in 1989 for two years of restoration work. It reopened in 1991, restored once more to its former glory.

Raffles Hotel
⊠ 1 Beach Road
☎ (65) 6337 1886
📠 (65) 6339 7650
✏ raffles@raffles.com
💻 www.rafflesshotel.com
Ⓜ City Hall and then walk towards Beach Road

Bras Basah Road
The name of this street, running from Dhoby Ghaut to **Raffles Hotel**, literally means 'wet rice' and is so named because of the wet rice traders who used to transport their produce by boat up the Stamford Canal and then lay it out to dry on the banks.

Left: *Singapore's most famous landmark is the main building of Raffles Hotel, known as 'The Grand Old Lady of the East'.*

Above: *The shining white Anglican cathedral of St Andrew's, built between 1856 and 1861 for the British colonialists.*
Opposite: *The gilded* gopuram, *or entrance tower, of the Sri Thanda-yuthapani Temple.*
Below: *The Armen-ian Church of St Gregory the Illumi-nator in Hill Street.*

Places of Worship
St Andrew's Cathedral

Designed by Colonel Ronald MacPherson, the cathedral was built using convict labour. The material used for the interior plaster is 'Madras chunam': shell lime, egg white and sugar, mixed with water and coconut husk and polished to a rocky white gloss.
⊠ *Coleman Street,*
☎ *(65) 6337 6104,*
🖳 *www.livingstreams. org.sg/sac*
M *City Hall*

Armenian Church

Built in 1835 and designed by George Coleman, the oldest church in Singapore is the Armenian Church of St Gregory the Illu-minator. Its imposing white portico is sup-ported by colonnades, flanked by balustrades and crowned with a tall spire. Important members of the Armenian community include the Sarkies brothers, who built Raffles Hotel, and Agnes Joachim, whose name was adopted for the national flower of Singapore, the Vanda 'Miss Joachim' (*see* panel, page 40).
⊠ *60 Hill Street,*
☎ *(65) 6334 0141,*
🖷 *(65) 6334 3279,*
⌂ *armen60@ singnet.com.sg*
M *City Hall*

Sacred Heart Church

The pillared interior walls and peculiar cor-ners of this church have given rise to the popular suspicion that it was built inside out in error.
⊠ *111 Tank Road,*
☎ *(65) 6737 9285,*
M *City Hall*

Sri Thandayutha-pani Temple

Known as the Hindu Chettiars' Temple, it was financed by the Chettiars, wealthy money-lenders from Madras who settled in Singapore. The temple is notable for its 48 engraved glass panels depicting deities, set into the roof at angles designed to catch the rising and setting sun. The temple has many magnificent statues and shrines dedicated to members of the Hindu pantheon, including the 120cm (4ft) peacock statue with a solid gold cobra coiled around it. Besides being the ultimate destination of the annual Thaipusam procession (see page 75), it is also the focal point for the celebration of the Navarathiri festival. Classical Indian music and dance are performed here over nine nights in October.

⊠ 15 Tank Road,

☎ (65) 6737 9393,

✆ (65) 6735 0804

M Dhoby Ghaut

Hong San See Chinese Temple

Now gazetted as a national monument, this temple is sited facing the water and backed by a hill, and is therefore believed to have very good feng shui (see panel, page 36). The temple is dedicated to the god of filial piety, a duty which is of paramount importance in Chinese society. It is said that the deity sold himself into slavery to pay for the upkeep of his parents' graves.

⊠ 31 Mohamed Sultan Road,

☎ (65) 737 3683,

M Dhoby Ghaut

Fuk Tak Ch'i Temple

This temple, known as 'The Temple of Prosperity and Virtue', was constructed in 1820 and rebuilt in 1825 as a Shentoist temple – Shentoism is a combination of Buddhism, Confucianism and Taoism. Here spiritual contacts with the dead can be channelled through the temple mediums. This Hakka temple is dedicated to Tua Pek Kong, the God of Wealth, whose statue is arrayed in sackcloth and his lips smeared with opium.

⊠ Telok Ayer Street,

M Raffles Place

Feng Shui

Feng shui, literally the science of wind and water, is central to the art of geomancy. It studies the harmony of cosmic elements on the sites of buildings, with the aim of attracting good luck and also dispelling bad. It continues to be a very important factor in the siting, size and design of Chinese buildings and their furnishings.

Opposite: *The beautiful Sultan Mosque, principal place of worship for Singapore's Muslim population.*

Below: *The Thian Hock Keng Temple, Singapore's oldest Chinese temple, was built by Hokkien immigrants grateful for a safe voyage.*

Thian Hock Keng Temple

Built in 1841, the 'Temple of Heavenly Happiness' is dedicated to Ma Chor Por, the Protector of Sailors. A pair of stone lions guards the entrance: twirl the stone ball in the mouth of the lion for good luck as you step over the high door sill which is built in this way to prevent evil spirits from entering. The inner altar is dedicated to Kuan Yin, the Goddess of Mercy, while smaller shrines are devoted to deities, including one featuring statues of horses where devotees pray for good fortune at the races. It is the oldest Chinese temple in Singapore and has been designated a national monument.

⊠ *158 Telok Ayer Street,*
☎ *(65) 6423 4616,*
📠 *(65) 6423 4626,*
M *Raffles Place or Tanjong Pagar*

Hajjah Fatimah Mosque

This tranquil mosque was built in 1846 by its namesake, a Melakan-born Malay who married a wealthy Bugis merchant. She amassed a fortune after her husband's death from her astute management of his shipping business, and built the mosque in the grounds of her home after she had moved away from the area. Hajjah Fatimah's tomb, together with that of her daughter Raja Sitti and her son-in-law Syed Ahmad Alsagoff, lies in the grounds of the mosque which today is taken care of by the Alsagoff family.

⊠ *4001 Beach Road,*
M *Lavender*

Sultan Mosque

Arab Street is dominated by the Sultan Mosque, the focal point of Islamic Singapore. Built in 1928 to a design by the colonial firm of Swan and Maclaren, who were also the architects for the Victoria Memorial Hall, it replaced the original 1820s mosque on this site. Its massive golden dome and huge prayer hall make it one of Singapore's most imposing religious buildings. During Ramadan the streets around the mosque take on a carnival atmosphere as hundreds of stalls sell delicacies with which Muslims break their fast each dusk.

✉ *3 Muscat Street,*
☎ *(65) 6293 4405,*
M *Bugis*

Temple of 1000 Lights

This simple Buddhist temple is also called the Sakaya Muni Buddha Gaya Temple. Its focal point is a 15m (50ft) seated Buddha surrounded by a huge number of light bulbs. Frescoes depicting the life of Buddha are etched at the base of the giant statue. Don't miss the secret reclining Buddha hidden away in an underground alcove accessed by a short flight of stairs at the back of the shrine beneath the seated Buddha.

✉ *366 Race Course Road,* ☎ *(65) 6294 0714,* **M** *Dhoby Ghaut and then take a taxi to the temple.*

Museums and Galleries
Singapore History Museum

Built in 1887, it houses a repository of Singapore's culture heritage, including examples of Peranakan culture and Williams Faquhar's collection of drawings. The museum traces the island's ethnic and religious diversity and has various historical artefacts and documents pertaining to its past.

✉ *30 Merchant Road, #03-09/17 Riverside Point,* ☎ *(65) 6332*

Jurong Crocodile Paradise

Situated next door to Jurong Bird Park, this crocodile farm is certainly no paradise for the reptiles, which are reared for their skin. While waiting for the inevitable in 'death row', the creatures are reluctant foils for the keepers' performances in death-defying acts of crocodile wrestling and handling. The farm has over 2500 crocodiles living in a faithful recreation of their natural habitat, with an underwater viewing gallery and breeding enclosures where nests of eggs are fiercely guarded by their mothers. Whilst the crocodile skins are used for making handbags and shoes, the crocodile meat ends up on the menu of the restaurant in the main entrance building. The Chinese people credit crocodile meat with medicinal value, especially in the treatment of asthma. The farm is open daily from 09:00 to 18:00; check the times for shows and feeding locally.

Opposite: *The Chinese Garden, on an island in Jurong Lake, is dotted with buildings in the style of the Sung Dynasty.*

3659 or 6332 3251,
🖳 *www.museum. org.sg/SHM*
M *Clarke Quay*
🕒 *Mon 13:00–19:00, Tue–Sun 09:00–19:00, Fri until 21:00*
🐷 *adults SG$2.00, children and senior citizens SG$1.00; free entry Fri after 19:00*

Singapore Art Museum

This museum was opened in 1996 in a building converted from the former St Joseph's Institution, which was built in 1855. It now houses the largest permanent collection of Southeast Asian modern and contemporary art pieces. There are more than 4000 pieces on display.
✉ *71 Bras Basah Rd,*
☎ *(65) 6332 3222,*
📠 *(65) 6334 7919,*
🖳 *www.museum.org. sg/sam/sam.html*
🕒 *10:00–19:00 daily, until 21:00 Fri*
🐷 *adults SG$3.00, students and senior citizens SG$1.50, family ticket (max. 5 members) SG$8.00;*

free admission Fri 18:00–21:00.
M *Dhoby Ghaut and City Hall*

Singapore Mint Coin Gallery

This is the numismatic museum of Singapore, where coins, medals and medallions from all over the world are displayed. Visitors can mint their own souvenir coin in the gallery's coin press.
✉ *20 Teban Gardens Crescent,*
☎ *(65) 6566 2626,*
📠 *(65) 6565 2626 or 6567 2626,*
🖎 *salesadmin@ singaporemint.com.sg*
🖳 *www. singapore mint.com.sg/*
🕒 *Mon–Fri 09:00– 16:30*
🐷 *SG$1.00, booking is required.*
M *Boon Lay*

Green Spaces
Marina City Park

This seafront park, south of the river and easily accessible from Marina Bay MRT, affords the visitor a splendid view of the

sea. Some of the features of the breezy promenade are an enormous sundial and a modern sculpture made of discs which revolve in the wind like a giant wind-chime. It is a popular venue for kite-flying while the calm waters are used for training by local rowing clubs and crews practising for the Dragon Boat Race (see page 42).
⊠ *Marina South,*
🖥 *www.nparks.gov.sg/parks/loc/par-loc-mar_cit.shtml*
M *Marina Bay*
🍽 *There are a good number of restaurants in the area.*

Chinese and Japanese Gardens

These two tranquil gardens are set on adjacent islands in Jurong Lake, and are linked by the 'Bridge of Double Beauty'. They exemplify the contrasting garden architecture of the two cultures. The Chinese Garden, known locally as **Yu**

Hwa Yuan, is fashioned after an imperial Sung dynasty design and mimics the grandeur of the Beijing Summer Palace. The landscape includes ornamental buildings with poetic names like 'Cloud-Piercing Pagoda', 'Moon-Receiving Tower' and 'Jade-Splashed Bridge'. Streams and pools such as the 'Fragrance-Filled Lily Pond' are dotted with vermilion and gold pavilions and stone boats. It is a firm favourite for bridal photographs.

By contrast, the Japanese Garden or **Seiwaen**, the 'Garden of Tranquillity', is refreshingly serene. Carp ponds are spanned by

Birds of Singapore
A March 1991 national bird census carried out by the Bird Group of the Nature Society of Singapore revealed 12,000 birds in areas like Marina South, Punggol, the Kranji bund and the offshore islands of Sentosa and St John's. Over 300 species have been recorded here. At the bird sanctuary at Sungei Buloh, on the northern coast, migrant birds including terns, egrets, plovers, herons and the Asiatic dowitcher can be seen in the mangrove swamps and ponds.

Singapore's National Flower

As well as several orchids that grow naturally on Singapore, an enormous number of species and hybrids are nurtured here. The orchidarium at the Botanic Gardens includes some rareties among its 250 varieties, as well as the Vanda Miss Joachim. This bright purple hybrid, which was chosen as the 'national flower' in 1981, was found in the garden of Agnes Joachim as a chance seedling in 1893.

Right: *Most of Singapore's natural rainforest disappeared a long time ago to make way for agriculture and urban development on this small, densely populated island. However, a few small pockets of primary vegetation remain and 81ha (200 acres) are protected in the Bukit Timah Nature Reserve, in the hilly centre of the island. Jungle trails wind through the forest beneath the towering canopy, enlivened by shimmering butterflies, exotic birds, monkeys and lemurs.*

wooden bridges, the landscape is traversed by pebble footpaths and stone lanterns are carefully placed among the shrubberies.

✉ *1 Chinese Garden,*
☎ *(65) 6261 3632,*
📠 *(65) 6261 1390,*
M *Chinese Garden*

Bukit Timah Nature Reserve

This rainforest reserve covering 81ha (200 acres) is one of only two of its kind in the world (the other being in Rio de Janeiro) in that it lies within the boundaries of a city. You can hike through the jungle along well-marked trails best tackled in the cool morning air and wearing sensible walking shoes. Those with keen eyes and ears will be rewarded by the sight of brilliant butterflies flitting among the thick foliage, exotic birds winging freely in the green canopy or inquisitive monkeys peering from the branches. Squirrels and lemurs are among the other wildlife found here. Unusual plants, such as the insect-eating pitcher plants, can be found here and there in the lush greenery. At the heart of the reserve rises Bukit Timah, the highest point in Singapore at a height of 165m (542ft). The reserve is open daily.

Left: *Fifteen golf courses and a number of driving ranges cater for the many keen golfers in Singapore – both locals and visitors.*

ACTIVITIES
Sport and Recreation

For the sports lover, Singapore offers excellent facilities for all major sports. There are fifteen **golf** courses to choose from. All except Tanah Merah Country Club permit non-members to play, though weekends are usually reserved for members and most clubs require visitors to hold a handicap or proficiency certificate from a recognized club. A number of driving ranges are available for practice. Opening hours for golf clubs are normally 07:00 to 19:00; some offer night golfing until 23:00.

For **bowling**, contact the Singapore Tenpin Bowling Congress (*see* panel, page 42). Most of the bowling centres open at 09:00 and close about 01:00 or 02:00. Prices are higher after 18:00 and at weekends and public holidays.

For the **water sports** enthusiast there is canoeing at Changi Point, East Coast Park and Sentosa Island, as well as scuba diving, windsurfing, sailing, water-skiing and swimming (most of the big hotels have pools; *see also* panel, page 43).

Tanglin Golf Course
✉ Minden Road
(5 holes, 668m, Par 15)
☎ (65) 6473 7236
🕐 daily 07:00–19:00
💰 weekdays SG$10.00 for 2 rounds, weekends and public holidays SG$15.00 for 2 rounds. Walk-in bookings. Golf cart/buggy and rental of golf equipment not available.

Green Fairways
✉ 60 Fairways Drive, off Eng Neo Avenue
(9 holes, 1887m, Par 32)
☎ (65) 6468 7233
📠 (65) 6468 7047
✉ www.turfclub.com.sg
🕐 daily 06:45–17:35
💰 weekdays SG$40.00 for 9 holes, SG$60.00 for 18 holes; weekends and public holidays SG$50.00 for 9 holes, SG$80.00 for 18 holes; golf cart: SG$3.10; golf club rental: SG$15.40–24.75. Proficiency or handicap certificates required. Walk-in bookings.
🍴 Cafeteria.

Above: *The 'Garden City' of Singapore is full of green oases among its densely packed buildings.*

Bowling
Singapore Tenpin Bowling Congress,
✉ 15 Stadium Road, National Stadium, Singapore 397718,
☎ (65) 6440 7388,
📠 (65) 6440 7488.

Cycling
Coastal Recreation Pte Ltd
✉ 1 East Coast Parkway, Singapore 1544,
☎ (65) 6448 7120.

Singapore Sports Council
✉ National Stadium, Kallang, Singapore 397718
☎ (65) 6345 7111,
📠 (65) 6340 9573,
🖥 www.ssc.gov.sg

Cycling is one of the Singaporeans' favourite pastimes. Bicycles can be hired at Coastal Recreation in East Coast Parkway (near the Food Centre), or at kiosks in Pasir Ris Park, Bishan Park and others, as well as near the Pulau Ubin jetty point and at Sentosa Island Bicycle Station (near the ferry terminal, at Siloso Beach, and at Palawan Beach).

The **Singapore Sports Council** exists to promote sports and physical fitness by planning, developing and maintaining public sports facilities. For further information on sports and recreation contact the Council – *see* panel, this page.

Dragon Boat Festival

This festival falls on the fifth day of the fifth lunar month (in June) to commemorate the death of Qu Yuan, a Chinese poet and statesman of the 4th century BC, who drowned himself in protest against political corruption. Fishermen raced in their boats to save him but they were too late. The people made glutinous rice dumplings with savoury meat fillings wrapped in bamboo leaves called *bah chang* and threw them in the river to distract the fish from eating his body. Since then, on the anniversary of his death, this gesture has been re-enacted with a boat race – now called 'The World Invitational Dragon Boat Race' – in Marina Bay, in which teams from all over the world compete. Stalls around the bay sell rice dumplings and souvenirs.

Singapore Turf Club

This famous race course, reputedly the best in the region, covers 140ha (350 acres) of hillocks and valleys. Two race tracks run 32 race days a year, commanding crowds of over 26,000 at each event. The prestigious Singapore Gold Cup is the main event in the racing calendar, followed by other races such as the Gold Cup, Singapore Derby, Lion City Cup, Raffles Cup, Queen Elizabeth II Cup and the Pesta Sukan Cup. Prize money ranges from S$150,000 to S$700,000. Apart from racing, the club has restaurants, a pub and food court, a jogging track, golf course and driving range, plus the first public riding school in Singapore. On non-racing days, turf events from Ipoh, Kuala Lumpur and Penang are telecast live on giant

Jalan Besar Swimming Complex
✉ 100 Tyrwhitt Road, #01-03, Singapore 207542,
☎ (65) 6293 9058.
M Lavender, then take service number 130.
🕐 08:00–21:30 daily
💰 weekdays: adults SG$1.00, children SG$0.50; weekends: adults SG$1.30, children SG$0.70
🍴 Snack bar is located within premises

Delta Swimming Complex
✉ 900 Tiong Bahru Road (158790)
☎ (65) 6474 7573
🕐 08.00–21:30 daily
💰 weekdays: adults SG$1.00, children SG$0.50; weekends: adults SG$1.30, children SG$0.70
M Redhill
🚌 32, 33, 63, 64, 132, 145
🍴 Snack bar located within the premises.

Left: *Insistent drumbeats urge on the competitors in the annual Dragon Boat Race in Marina Bay.*

Snow City
✉ 321 Jurong Town
Hall Road
☎ (65) 6337 1511,
📠 (65) 6338 1500,
🕐 09:00–20:30
Tue–Sun, closed Mon
except for school and
public holidays.

screens. Tours of the race course are available, including a buffet lunch and entrance to the members' enclosure.

Spectator Sports

For those who would rather watch than play, details of sporting fixtures can be found in the daily press. The **Singapore Cricket Club** holds matches on the Padang at weekends from March to October. Rugby is played here for the rest of the year. There are regular polo matches from February to October at the Singapore Polo Club in Mount Pleasant Road. Football is played at regional stadiums around the island. Singapore has its own professional league, called S–League. The Formula One Powerboat Grand Prix is held in Marina Bay in November each year.

Singapore Surprise

Snow is probably the very last thing you would expect to encounter in hot and sunny Singapore. At **Snow City**, however,

Below: *Singapore Cricket Club, at one end of the Padang, is the venue for most big sporting events in the city as well as National Day parades.*

there is abundant snow. The temperature is kept at a constant -5°C (23°F) in the indoor snow chamber, where you can enjoy skiing, snowboarding and snowtubing – there is also a play area for snowball fighting.

Above: *Boat Quay, one of the main attractions of the Waterfront area.*

Snow City provides visitors with boots, jackets and snow tubes, the use of which is included in the admission charge.

Walking Tour
The Waterfront

The waterfront of Singapore has borne silent witness to the trials and tribulations of a developing nation. When Stamford Raffles landed in 1819, there was already some activity in the small farming settlement of Malays and Chinese. It was also infested with Bugis pirates who were said to have littered the area with the dead bodies of their victims. A lesser man might have been deterred by this macabre environment.

Today, the only invaders are tourists and the area is not even littered with rubbish, but the bustling atmosphere remains – the place is full of noise, people and colour. The old godowns and warehouses have been lovingly restored and converted into discos, bars, shops and restaurants, particularly along **Clarke** and **Boat Quays** (*see* page 18). Bumboats still chug along the river ferrying passengers on joyrides and river cruises. Singapore has prospered but it has not quite forgotten its humble beginnings.

> **A Walk Around the Waterfront**
> **Location:** Map F–D4
> **Distance:** about 1.5km (1 mile)
> **Duration:** about an hour, including stops
> **Start:** Raffles Place MTR station
> **Finish:** One Fullerton

Above: *The statue of the mythical Merlion stands guard at the mouth of the Singapore River.*
Opposite: *Cruises to the southern islands depart from the World Trade Centre.*

It has restored the riverside to its former thriving state, albeit in a somewhat sanitized state for the tourists.

Alight from Raffles Place MRT (Map F–D4) and take a stroll towards the waterfront through Change Alley, once a popular bazaar for bargain-hunting, to Collyer Quay. A pedestrian bridge, called **Change Alley Aerial Plaza**, a cleaned-up version of the once bustling bazaar full of money-changers and tailors, cuts across to **Clifford Pier**, from which Chinese junks and pleasure boats depart to take tourists on harbour cruises or trips to the southern islands. To the south, towards the business district of Shenton Way and Robinson Road (Map F–C5), is the **Lau Pa Sat Festival Market** (formerly Telok Ayer Market) in Boon Tat Street. Built in 1894, this ornate building is the last remaining Victorian filigree cast-iron structure in Southeast Asia. It was once a wet market and a food centre. It was dismantled during the building of the MRT and has been restored and converted into a festival market with shops, live entertainment and food centres serving local fare. In the evening, Boon Tat Street is closed to traffic and taken over by alfresco eating places. The market is open from 07:00 to 00:00.

A walk heading to the north up Fullerton Road will bring you to **Merlion Park** (Map F–D3) and the water-spouting statue of the

Merlion, a mythical beast with the head of a lion and the body of a fish. Created in 1972 and installed at the mouth of the Singapore River, it has become not only the symbol of tourism in Singapore, but also the national emblem.

Connaught Drive, across the Anderson Bridge, has a park skirting the Padang (Map F–D2) and affording a scenic view of the sea. Along Fullerton Road is **One Fullerton**, a complex of upmarket eateries and nightclubs with a generous view of Marina Bay. From here, you will also be able to see the **Esplanade-Theatres On The Bay** (see page 29), two dome-like structures that house some world-class performance venues. The locals affectionately refer to the Esplanade as the Durians, after their favourite pungent spikey fruit.

Organized Tours

Singapore's tour operators offer a wide variety of organized trips around the city, either for general sightseeing or with a special interest. Evening tours include a

Tour Operators
Holiday Tours and Travel, ✉ 300 Orchard Rd, The Promenade, ☎ (65) 6738 2622, 📠 6733 3226.
RMG Tours, ✉ 109C Amoy St, ☎ (65) 6220 1661, 📠 6324 6530.
Siakson Coach Tours, ☎ (65) 6331 8201, 📠 6337 4814.
SH Tours, ☎ (65) 6734 9923, 📠 6738 7955.
Singapore Sightseeing Tour East, ☎ (65) 6735 1221, ✉ temice@ singnet.com.sg

River and Island Cruises
Singapore River Cruises, ☎ (65) 6336 6111, 📠 6336 6112.
Singapore Explorer, ☎ (65) 6339 6833.
Ananda Travel, ☎ (65) 6732 1766.
Fantasy Cruises, ☎ (65) 6283 2182, 📠 382 5293.

Singapore Discovery Centre

✉ 510 Upper Jurong Road

☎ (65) 6792 6188

📠 (65) 6792 1233

🖥 www.sdc.com.sg/

🕘 09:00–19:00 Tue–Sun, last admission at 18:00.

💰 adults SG$9.00, children SG$5.00, senior citizens SG$6.00

Ⓜ Boon Lay, then take SBS Bus no. 182/193 from Boon Lay Bus Interchange and alight at Singapore Discovery Centre.

Singapore Science Centre

✉ 15 Science Centre Road

☎ (65) 6425 2500

📠 (65) 6565 9533

🖥 www.science.edu. sg/ssc/index.jsp

🕘 10:00–18:00 Tue–Sun, closed Mon except school and public holidays; last admission 17:15, Omnimax Theatre's last movie screening 20:00

💰 adults SG$6.00, children SG$3.00, senior citizens SG$3.60; separate admission fees for entrance to the museum, the Omnimax Theatre and the Planetarium Show (check the times of shows locally).

Ⓜ Jurong East

meal, usually at an open-air food centre. Bookings can be made with the companies or through your hotel tour desk. There is also a wide choice of tours outside the city: numerous sightseeing and special interest tours are available, and these can be booked either through your hotel or with one of the companies listed (*see* panel, page 47). Here are a few interesting suggestions: Round Island Tours; Night Safari (three-hour tour including a tram ride); Singapore by Night; Helicopter Sightseeing Tour; Sentosa Tour.

At the southernmost tip of the island, directly opposite Sentosa, lies the focal point of all the maritime activities of Singapore. The World Trade Centre adjoining the **Singapore Cruise Centre** is the departure point for the cruise liners and ferries that make their way to Indonesia and also to the islands of Singapore. The whole World Trade Centre complex also doubles as a family fun centre and entertainment plaza, with various attractions and amenities that include an amphitheatre, restaurants, shops, travel agents and banks. Dining or strolling along the breezy **Harbour Promenade** affords a view of the busy port: blasts from their horns announce the ships' departures and catamarans skim over the ocean to distant islands.

Fun for Children

Singapore's achievements and technological progress are charted at the **Singapore Discovery Centre**. The distinctive feature of this high-technology, interactive attraction is that it allows the visitor get up close and personal with a number of very interesting

science experiments. (While you're in the area, you can also pay a visit to the Omni-Theatre which offers a 3D cinematic experience on its 23m (75ft) wide screen.)

The **Singapore Science Centre**, a 'hands-on' museum with around 600 exhibits and interactive displays, brings fun and entertainment to the world of science. It is chiefly aimed at children, many of whom visit the centre in school parties, but in fact its imaginative explanations of scientific principles are just as appealing to adults. Its highlights include the **Aviation Gallery** which charts the history and principles of flight; the **Omnimax Theatre** which gives the viewer a virtual reality experience of the films projected on its massive hemispherical screen with special sound effects; and the **Planetarium Show** taking visitors on an excursion around the solar system.

Above: *Singapore Science Centre, with interactive activities illustrating the wonders of technology, is a great day out for children.*

Above: *Ngee Ann City is an enormous shopping centre in Orchard Road.*
Opposite: *Lucky Plaza is very popular with the tourists.*

Ngee Ann City
Reputedly the largest shopping centre in Southeast Asia, Ngee Ann City's striking architecture is a landmark in Orchard Road. Its six floors are packed with merchandise and include high fashion boutiques and Tiffany's. Its anchor tenant, Takashimaya, features a department store, cultural facilities, specialist shops, restaurants, a health club, a swimming pool and function halls.
⊠ 391 Orchard Road,
☎ (65) 6739 9323,
M Orchard (NS22)

Shopping

Singapore has long been acknowledged as a wonderful place to shop and indeed travellers from all over the world make a point of stopping over in the city to snap up a bargain or two. The air-conditioning and the state-of-the-art window displays are added attractions. Although prices are not as competitive as they once were, there are still bargains to be had. **Orchard Road** is the main shopping district of Singapore where department stores and shops line each side of the street.

Shopping Centres

Tangs
Five floors of shops; a variety of goods from household to fashion and electronic items.
⊠ 320 Orchard Road,
☎ (65) 6737 5500,
M Orchard (NS22)

Centrepoint
Consumer goods such as fashions, furniture, stationery, toys, sports equipment and books.
⊠ 176 Orchard Road,
☎ (65) 6737 9000.

Far East Plaza
Popular with locals for bargain hunting.
⊠ 14 Scotts Road,
☎ (65) 6734 2325.

Far East Shopping Centre

Jewellery, health equipment, jade sculptures and ivory carvings.
✉ 545 Orchard Road,
☎ (65) 6734 5541.

Lucky Plaza

Sells everything: electronic goods, watches, clothes and jewellery.
✉ 304 Orchard Road,
☎ (65) 6235 3294.

Midpoint Orchard

Sporting goods, gold jewellery, bridal gowns, fur coats and jackets.
✉ 220 Orchard Road,
Ⓜ Somerset (NS23)

OG Building

A good selection of footwear and clothes.
✉ 228 Orchard Road,
☎ (65) 6737 4488,
Ⓜ Somerset (NS23)

Orchard Plaza

A choice of electronic goods and cameras.
✉ 150 Orchard Road,
Ⓜ Somerset (NS23)

Orchard Towers

Another good place for electronic and photographic goods.

✉ 600 Orchard Road,
Ⓜ Orchard (NS22)

The Shaw Centre

Fashion, jewellery, shoes and accessories.
✉ 1 Scotts Road,
☎ (65) 6737 9080.

Shaw House (Isetan)

The well-stocked Japanese department store sells sushi and other delicious items.
✉ 350 Orchard Road,
☎ (65) 6235 1150.
Ⓜ Orchard (NS22)

Specialist's Shopping Centre

Home to John Little, one of Singapore's oldest established department stores. Speciality shops sell everything from Famous Amos cookies to golf equipment. The Korean restaurant on level five was the first Korean restaurant in Singapore.
✉ 277 Orchard Road,
☎ (65) 6737 8222,
Ⓜ Somerset (NS23)

Paragon

Here you will find mostly designer clothes from the West and also some local couturiers.
✉ 290 Orchard Road,
☎ (65) 6738 5535,
Ⓜ Orchard (NS22)

The Jewels of Little India

Gold and silver jewellery have always played an important part in Indian culture, not just as a measurement of wealth or as dowries for women, but also for religious purposes. The streets in Little India are thronged with shops displaying a dazzling array of jewels. Some sell silver sheets embossed with parts of the body, to be used as temple offerings when seeking a cure for a specific ailment. Silver amulets are worn for luck and protection from evil spirits, while fine silver spears are used to pierce the bodies of devotees in a Thaipusam procession. Heavy ropes of sovereign coins strung on ornate chains are popular for dowries. Encrusted earrings with long chains with hooks on each end are worn by Indian women with the chain hooked into the hair as a traditional dual-purpose accessory. Gold jewellery in Singapore is of 22 or 24 carat and is priced according to the weight of gold and the design of the piece. Current market prices for gold are usually displayed on a board in the shop; when a buyer selects a piece of jewellery, the goldsmith will weigh it and charge accordingly.

Palais Renaissance

This imposing complex houses a superb range of prestigious designer boutiques including DKNY, Gianni Versace, Prada, The Link and Jim Thompson.

✉ 390 Orchard Road,
M Orchard (NS22)

Tudor Court

This charming row of Tudor-front shops offers the shopper a variety of antiques and home furnishings.

✉ 131 Tanglin Road,
M Orchard (NS22)

Tanglin Shopping Centre

This is the place for antiques and exquisite oriental treasures. Antique maps and prints are specialities here, as are intricately woven oriental carpets. Mata-Hari Antiques and Ken Soon Asiatic Art sell souvenirs, arts and crafts.

✉ 19 Tanglin Road,
☎ (65) 6737 0849,
M Orchard (NS22)

Plaza Singapura

This was the first multi-storey shopping mall in Singapore, built in 1974. It has cinemas, fashion, music, home furnishing and a wide range of food outlets. It will soon be linked with the Dhoby Ghaut MRT station, the new north-east MRT-line interchange and SMRT Light Rail line to the downtown Civic and Business District.

✉ 68 Orchard Road,
☎ (65) 6332 9298,
M Dhoby Ghaut

Useful Shopping Tips

• Though haggling is a way of life in Singapore, it is mostly confined to smaller outlets, markets, bazaars and shops where the window sticker says 'recommended prices'. Most of the larger outlets have fixed prices.

• To take advantage of the tax refund for visitors (*see page 90*), be sure to buy from shops displaying the tax refund logo and remember to obtain the relevant form from the retailer.

• For electronic and electrical goods, check the compatibility of voltage and cycle at home: you may need an adaptor.

• Make sure you get an international warranty and receipt for cameras, watches and electrical goods.

• When arranging for goods to be sent to your home, always ask for written confirmation from the shop or factory.

• Shops are generally open from 10:00 to 21:00.

• Be careful when buying items on sale, since these are often non-exchangeable or refundable. Alterations to sale items are also often suspended.

• If you have any shopping grievance, you can seek redress from the **Retail Promotion Centre** (☎ 6450 2114) or the **Small Claims Tribunal** (✉ #05-00, Apollo Centre, 2 Havelock Road, ☎ 6435 3375).

• Free online dispute resolution service is available at E@DR Centre, ✉ www. e-adr.org.sg

Above: *A shopkeeper sits in one of Little India's five-foot ways.*
Opposite: *Dazzling Malay outfits fill a Geylang Serai shop.*

The Art of Batik

Batik is usually made from cotton or silk. Traditional motifs include flowers and stylized animals, created by the application of wax to the required design, dyeing, drying and repeating the process with different coloured dyes until the pattern is complete over the whole length of fabric. It is a laborious process and takes hours of patience and deft hands. The end results are used for clothing, wall hangings, scarves, sarongs, handbags, tablecloths, placemats and other accessories. Batik and silk are good buys in Arab Street.

Right: *After a two-year restoration programme which sought to recreate the hotel's heyday in the 1920s, Raffles is once more the last word in luxury.*

Rival Hotels

'Feed at Raffles – where the food is excellent.' This ringing endorsement from the young Rudyard Kipling was enthusiastically taken up by Tigran Sarkies in the late 1880s. However, the article from which he extracted it was not so wholehearted in its praise: 'Providence conducted me along a beach, in full view of five miles of shipping – five solid miles of masts and funnels – to a place called Raffles Hotel, where the food is excellent as the rooms are bad. Let the traveller take note. Feed at Raffles and sleep at the Hotel de l'Europe.'

Work began on extensions to Raffles to improve the accommodation in 1890. The elegant Hotel de l'Europe was demolished to make way for the Supreme Court building in 1936.

WHERE TO STAY

Accommodation in Singapore ranges from ultra luxury world-class hotels to humble inns and guesthouses, thereby catering for the budget of every traveller. Singapore boasts a very high standard of hotels and generally good value for money. All the upscale five- and four-star hotels offer spacious accommodation with modern facilities in prime locations, a wide choice of food and beverage outlets, swimming pools, as well as business and conference facilities with sleek, efficient service. Lower mid-range hotels, especially those converted from old shophouses, are chic and present a boutique-style ambience with all the mod cons and food outlets, some even with swimming pools. There is a plethora of low budget hotels and hostels offering clean, comfortable rooms with basic amenities and limited outlets, some with shared bathrooms while others may even have en suite bathrooms. Most hotels in Singapore are equipped with broadband Internet facilities.

Singapore

• *LUXURY*

The Fullerton Hotel

(Map F–D3)

A world class hotel converted from an historical landmark building with neo-classical architecture built in 1928, with spacious and modern rooms. Excellent location to explore the Civic district, museums and waterfront.

✉ *1 Fullerton Square,*
☎ *(65) 6733 8388,*
📠 *(65) 6735 8388,*
🖰 *info@*
fullertonhotel.com
🖥 *www.*
fullertonhotel.com

Raffles Hotel

(Map F–E1)

The most famous historical landmark in Singapore which has served as a hotel since 1887. It has evolved into an all-suite hotel favoured by celebrities, writers and royalty.

✉ *1 Beach Road,*
☎ *(65) 6337 1886,*
📠 *(65) 6339 7650,*
🖰 *raffles@raffles.com*
🖥 *www.*
raffleshotel.com

Four Seasons Hotel Singapore

(Map H–B2)

Situated near the financial district and just round the corner from the main shopping avenues in Orchard Road, the Four Seasons Hotel Singapore is lavishly furnished with lovely oriental antiques and works of art. The restaurants are excellent, and there are great facilities for keeping fit.

✉ *190 Orchard Boulevard,*
☎ *(65) 6734 1110,*
📠 *(65) 6733 0682,*
🖰 *businesscentre.sin@ fourseasons.com*
🖥 *www.fourseasons. com/singapore*

Intercontinental Singapore

(Map G–C5)

The Intercontinental Singapore is a modern hotel with a touch of old-world charm. It has its distinctive Peranakan architecture, is located in the civic and cultural district of Singapore, and forms part of the Bugis Junction complex which has many bustling shops. The hotel has good fitness facilities, and the level of service is truly outstanding.

✉ *80 Middle Road,*
☎ *(65) 6338 7600,*
📠 *(65) 6338 7366,*
🖰 *singapore@ interconti.com*
🖥 *www. intercontinental.com*

The Regent Singapore

(Map H–B1)

The Regent is conveniently located in the city's business district and is just minutes away from Singapore's most exclusive shopping and entertainment hub – Orchard Road. Excellent rooms, a fully equipped business centre, and fine restaurants.

✉ *1 Cuscaden Road,*
☎ *(65) 6733 8888,*
📠 *(65) 6732 8838,*
🖰 *regent3@ magix.com.sg*
🖥 *www. regenthotels.com*

The Oriental Singapore

(Map G–A6)

Situated at the prime waterfront location adjacent to Suntec City convention centre, the Oriental Singapore commands city, ocean and harbour views from its spacious rooms and suites, and is within easy reach of riverside attractions.

✉ *5 Raffles Avenue, Marina Square,*
☎ *(65) 6338 0066,*
📠 *(65) 6339 9537,*
🖱 *orsin@mohg.com*
🖥 *www.mandarinoriental.com*

• UPPER MID-RANGE

Goodwood Park Hotel (Map H–C3)

A historical building within walking distance of Orchard Road and the city's financial district and night spots. It exudes old-world charm and elegance with a colonial air.

✉ *22 Scotts Road,*
☎ *(65) 6737 7411,*
📠 *(65) 6732 8558,*
🖱 *enquiries@good*
woodparkhotel.com
🖥 *www.goodwood parkhotel.com.sg*

Swissôtel The Stamford Singapore

(Map F–D1)

Located in the heart of Singapore amid the Raffles City Shopping Complex, this hotel houses the Equinox Complex – a unique collection of distinctive restaurants and stylish clubs located on the 70th and 72nd floors of the hotel, commanding a bird's-eye view of Singapore, which is especially spectacular at night.

✉ *2 Stamford Road,*
☎ *(65) 6338 8585,*
📠 *(65) 6338 2862,*
🖱 *emailus.singapore@ swissotel.com*
🖥 *www.swissotel-thestamford.com*

Royal Plaza On Scotts (Map H–C2)

The Royal Plaza Hotel is situated right in the centre of Singapore's bustling business, shopping and entertainment district. It is also just steps away from Orchard Road.

✉ *25 Scotts Road,*
☎ *(65) 6737 7966,*
📠 *(65) 6737 6646,*
🖱 *royal@royalplaza. com.sg*
🖥 *www. royalplaza.com.sg*

Pan Pacific Singapore

(Map G–C6)

Conveniently located next to Suntec City, the Pan Pacific Singapore Hotel is also connected to the Marina Square and Millenium Walk shopping centres, and is within easy access of many of Singapore's attractions. Good for business travellers.

✉ *7 Raffles Boulevard, Marina Square,*
☎ *(65) 6336 8111,*
📠 *(65) 6339 1861,*
🖱 *singapore@ panpacific.com*
🖥 *www.singapore. panpacific.com*

Grand Copthorne Waterfront Hotel

(Map F–A3)

Situated right on the banks of the

Singapore River, the Grand Copthorne Waterfront Hotel is within easy access of the shopping and entertainment areas of Chinatown and Orchard Road, and just minutes away from the central business district.

✉ *392 Havelock Road,*
☎ *(65) 6733 0880,*
📠 *(65) 6737 8880,*
📧 *grandcopthorne@ copthorne.com.sg*
🖥 *www.grand copthorne.com.sg*

Meritus Mandarin Singapore

(Map H–B4)
Situated right in the heart of Orchard Road, Singapore's premier shopping, entertainment and business district, and the location of some of the hottest night-spots in Singapore.

✉ *333 Orchard Road,*
☎ *(65) 6737 4411,*
📠 *(65) 6732 2361,*
📧 *mandarin.tms@ meritus-hotels.com*
🖥 *www.mandarin-singapore.com*

• *LOWER MID-RANGE*

Albert Court Hotel

(Map G–B3)
A charming boutique hotel conserved from prewar shophouses with a lean towards East and West décor and also a touch of Peranakan style. The hotel is situated in a quiet street near Little India.

✉ *180 Albert Street,*
☎ *(65) 6339 3939,*
📠 *(65) 6339 3252,*
📧 *info@albertcourt. com.sg*
🖥 *www. albertcourt.com.sg*

The Gallery Hotel

(Map F–A2)
The Gallery Hotel has styled itself as a hotel with post-modern architecture and colourful interiors. It is situated in the trendy Robertson Quay entertainment district on the Singapore River. As the name suggest, there's an art gallery. There is also an excellent restaurant and a glass, rooftop swimming pool.

Singapore's Founding Father

Seafaring was undoubtedly in Raffles' blood. The son of a sea-caption, Benjamin Raffles, he was born at sea on 6 July 1871 aboard his father's ship *Ann*. Benjamin Raffles died heavily in debt, so that Thomas was obliged to leave school at 14, but during his years as a clerk in the East India Company he continued to educate himself with fervour. He was an able historian and zoologist and published *A History of Java* in 1817, the year in which he was knighted. In that same year he had suggested to Sir Joseph Banks establishing a collection of animals in London. When he returned to live per-manently in England in 1824 he and Sir Humphrey Davy founded the Zoological Society of London, of which Raffles became the first president. He died in 1826, two days before his 45th birthday.

Tourism is fast becoming a major contributor to Singapore's growing economy. The STPB (Singapore Tourist Promotion Board) was formed in 1964 with the aim of attracting millions of visitors to Singapore annually. The average length of stay in Singapore is 3.7 days, but the STPB is committed to change its 'shop till you drop', stopover image and entice visitors to stay longer. A S$1 billion tourist facilities programme is in progress, and an earnest conservation project was launched in the 1980s, restoring landmarks such as Raffles Hotel, Chinatown and Little India. The STPB is also aggressively promoting Singapore as a world-class convention and exhibition centre: a S$13 million programme, 'Meet in Singapore 1995', was launched to coincide with the unveiling of the S$2 billion Suntech City – Singapore International Convention and Exhibition Centre.

✉ *76 Robertson Quay,* ☎ *(65) 6849 8686,*
📠 *(65) 6836 6666,*
🖰 *general@ galleryhotel.com.sg*
💻 *www. galleryhotel.com.sg*

Hotel 1929

(Map F–A5)
Situated right in the heart of Chinatown, this hotel was converted from old shophouses built in 1929 and transformed into a boutique hotel with chic and innovative modern interiors.
✉ *50 Keong Saik Road,*
☎ *(65) 6347 1929,*
📠 *(65) 6327 1929,*
🖰 *reservations@ hotel1929.com*
💻 *www. hotel1929.com*

The Royal Peacock Hotel (Map F–A5)

Located in the centre of Chinatown, the Royal Peacock Hotel was restored from ten shophouses, and was decorated with a burst of dark warm colours – note the red and purple tones in the corridors and the compact rooms.
✉ *55 Keong Saik Road,*
☎ *(65) 6223 3522,*
📠 *(65) 6221 1770,*
🖰 *rpeacock@ singnet.com.sg*
💻 *www.royal peacockhotel.com*

Berjaya Duxton Hotel (Map F–A5)

This small boutique hotel was converted from old shophouses situated within the Central Business District. It is within walking distance of the city centre and Chinatown.
✉ *83 Duxton Road,*
☎ *(65) 6227 7678,*
📠 *(65) 6227 1232,*
🖰 *berjayahotel@ pacific.net.sg*
💻 *www. berjayaresorts.com*

Plaza Park Royal

(Map G–E5)
Strategically located along the perimeters of the CBD and within close proximity of Singapore International Convention

and Exhibition Centre, The Plaza Park Royal also offers complimentary shuttle services to the major entertainment and shopping areas.

✉ 7500A Beach Road,
☎ (65) 6298 0011,
📠 (65) 6296 3600,
🖱 plaza@sin.
parkroyalhotels.com
🖥 www.plaza.
singapore.parkroyal
hotels.com

• LOW COST BUDGET HOTELS
Hangout@Mt.Emily
(Map H–C6)

Styled as a 'No frills – Just Fun' budget hotel with bright, comfortable rooms and hip interiors, this hotel caters mainly for younger travellers. Great value for money. Nearby Mt. Emily Park provides some tranquillity.

✉ 10A Upper Wilkie Road,
☎ (65) 6338 9151,
📠 (65) 6339 6008,
🖱 enquiries@
hangout-hotels.com
🖥 www.hangout-
hotels.com

Sloane Court Hotel
(Map H–C2)

Charming Tudor-style hotel with colonial charm, set in a residential area. Very friendly staff.

✉ 17 Balmoral Road,
☎ (65) 6235 3311,
📠 (65) 6733 9041,
🖱 sloane@
singnet.com.sg

The Inncrowd Bunk and Brekkie
(Map G–B3)

A friendly, cosy hostel located in Little India. This place has a homely atmosphere.

✉ 73 Dunlop Street,
☎ (65) 6296 9169,
🖱 inquiry@
the-inncrowd.com
🖥 www.the-
inncrowd.com

Perak Lodge
(Map G–B3)

Located in Little India within close proximity of main attractions.

✉ 12 Perak Road,
☎ (65) 6299 7733,
📠 (65) 6392 0919,
🖱 perlodge@
singnet.com.sg
🖥 www.
peraklodge.net

Strand Hotel
(Map G–A5)

Situated in the heart of the cultural, civic and commercial district and within walking distance of main attractions and Orchard Road.

✉ 25 Bencoolen Street,
☎ (65) 6338 1866,
📠 (65) 6338 1330,
🖱 reservations@
strandhotel.com.sg
🖥 www.
strandhotel.com.sg

Chinatown Hotel
(Map F–A5)

Conveniently located within the central business district, and a short distance to the civic centre, the restored shophouse hotel is set in the heart of Chinatown. The rooms have all the basics including TV and writing desk.

✉ 12–16 Teck Lim Road,
☎ (65) 6225 5166,
📠 (65) 6225 3912,
🖱 enquiries@
chinatownhotel.com
🖥 www.
chinatownhotel.com

No Durians Allowed

EATING OUT

To describe Singapore as a gourmet's paradise is not an exaggeration. It is a country where serious eating is a favourite pastime. Food centres and hawker stalls, which serve mostly fresh local fare, are very inexpensive, and what they lack in decor (not to mention air-conditioning) they make up for in local colour. Local dishes are a unique blend of **Malay**, **Indian**, **Chinese** and **Nyonya** cuisines. It is common practice to pay for your food and drinks when they are served. You can order from any stall as seats are shared between the vendors. Expect to pay more for food in air-conditioned restaurants, while hotel restaurants can be quite expensive. No smoking is allowed in any indoor restaurants in Singapore, though there is no restriction in alfresco eating-places.

Ethnic Cuisine
Chinese Food

Chinese cuisine is important in Singapore. Although most of the Chinese population originated from Fukien, Chinese food in Singapore is largely **Cantonese** in style. **Beijing** and spicy **Szechuan** dishes are also gaining in popularity, while the **Hainanese** are famous for their chicken rice.

In Chinese society, eating is more than the mere consumption of food. A Chinese banquet is a visual feast of colours and elaborate garnishes, and ingredients are combined to ensure harmony between the *yin* and *yang* qualities of the food. On festive occasions food is chosen for its symbolic associations. For example, noodles are a compulsory dish at birthdays to symbolize longevity, oysters bring good fortune to the Cantonese as their name also means 'good things' or 'business', and fish signifies prosperity.

Indian Food

Cuisines from India are well represented in Singapore. There is a choice of dishes, from fiery **southern Indian** curries enriched with coconut milk to creamy yoghurt-based dishes from the **Punjab**. Little India is noted for its vegetarian restaurants, while the more adventurous might want to sample the renowned fish-head curry, cooked with okra and brinjals and served with pickles and rice heaped high on a banana leaf. **Indian Muslims** serve their own speciality of *nasi biryani*, a saffron rice dish with spicy chicken or mutton, and *murtabak*, unleavened bread with minced meat and onions.

Malay/Indonesian Food

Malay food is spicy without necessarily being chilli hot, although this fiery spice is used in most dishes. It makes liberal use of coconut and local spices and sometimes borrows subtly from Indian cooking, as is evident in its **Korma** dishes of mild chicken curry and *nasik minyak*, rice cooked with spices and ghee. **Peanut sauce** plays a vital part in dishes like *gado gado*, an Indonesian salad comprising lettuce, bean sprouts and fried bean curd topped with peanut sauce. **Satay** – skewers of meat grilled over charcoal and then served with raw onions, fresh cucumber and *ketupat* (coconut rice

> ### What to Drink in Singapore
> Apart from water, which is perfectly safe to drink in Singapore (and therefore also safe as ice in drinks) thirst-quenchers in the tropical heat include:
> **Fruit juice:** many varieties are available freshly squeezed everywhere you go.
> **Tea:** this is always the perfect complement to Chinese food.
> **Beer:** the local brews are Tiger and Anchor. Western beers are widely available.
> Other local favourites are Malay *ayer bandung* (made with rose syrup and condensed milk) and soya bean milk. Wines, spirits and fizzy soft drinks are all easily available.

Opposite: *Passengers may not carry these malodorous fruit on board the MRT.*
Below: *Chilli crab is among the temptations offered at this night market stall.*

cubes) – are also accompanied by peanut sauce, as is *tauhu goreng*, fried bean curd stuffed with shredded raw vegetables. *Sambal belachan*, shrimp paste with chilli and lime, is eaten with raw vegetables or rice. If you are eating in a group it would be fun to try the *rijstafel*, which is a Dutch-Indonesian meal of rice and spicy dishes served in ten or twelve courses.

Malay and Indian foods are traditionally eaten with the fingertips of the right hand, but restaurants do provide eating implements for the uninitiated.

Nyonya Food

Nyonya (Peranakan) food is a blend of Malay and Chinese cooking, using local ingredients to produce one of the most exquisite cuisines of the region. Coconut, tamarind, lemon grass, shrimp paste and chilli form the basis of most of its dishes. A famous Nyonya dish is *laksa* (actually Indian in origin), rice vermicelli served in coconut milk and garnished with prawns, chicken and bean sprouts.

Other Cuisines

Singapore, with its cosmopolitan society, offers visitors a wide range of international cuisines from which to make their selection. From other countries in Asia come Thai, Korean, Japanese, Vietnamese and Mongolian restaurants, while virtually all types of western food are also served.

Below: *Laksa, a Nyonya speciality, forms the centrepiece of this feast.*

Singapore

• CHINESE

Ah Hoi's Kitchen

Nostalgic '60's Chinese cuisine.

✉ Traders Hotel,
1A Cuscaden Road,
☎ (65) 6831 4373.

Damenlou (Swee Kee Restaurant)

Specials: Fried chicken with prawn paste and beancurd in casserole.

✉ 12 Ann Siang Hill,
☎ (65) 6222 8926.

Prima Taste

A gathering of some of Singapore's best tasting dishes.

✉ Centrepoint, 176 Orchard Road,
☎ (65) 6887 3786, and
✉ One Fullerton,
☎ (65) 6438 8337.

Jing Signature Chinese Cuisine

Classical Chinese cuisine in a heritage site.

✉ 50 Eu Tong Sen St,
☎ (65) 6532 6006.

Lei Garden

Cantonese menu with more than 120 dishes.

✉ Chijmes, Victoria St, ☎ (65) 6339 3822.

Golden Peony

Innovation and Chinese cuisine meet.

✉ Conrad Centennial Hotel,
☎ (65) 6334 8888.

• INDIAN

Muthu's Curry

Famous fish head curry in authentic Indian style.

✉ Race Course Road,
☎ (65) 6293 2389.

Bukhara

Tandoor ovens in traditional Northwest Indian style.

✉ 87, Club Street,
☎ (65) 6323 4544.

Kinara

Spicy North Indian curries.

✉ 24 Lorong Mambong, Holland Village,
☎ (65) 6467 4101.

Komala Vilas

Vegetarian Indian.

✉ 12–14 Buffalo Road,
☎ (65) 6293 6980.

Vansh

Modish Indian cuisine served here.

✉ #01–04, Singapore Indoor Stadium, 2, Stadium Walk,
☎ (65) 6345 4466.

• MALAY AND INDONESIAN

Rendezvous

A legendary old favourite serving up Malay nasi padang.

✉ #02–03, Hotel Rendezvous, 9 Bras Basah Road,
☎ (65) 6339 7508.

Alkaff Mansion

Dutch-Indonesian rijstafel.

✉ 10, Telok Blangah Green,
☎ (65) 6278 6979.

• NYONYA

The Blue Ginger

A fusion of Chinese, Malay and European cultures has created the Peranakan cuisine known as Nyonya.

✉ 97 Tanjong Pagar Road,
☎ (65) 6222 3928.

Belachan

Traditional Straits Chinese fare.

✉ 10 Smith Street,
☎ (65) 6221 9810.

Nutmeg Trees

You would be hard pressed to find a nutmeg tree in Singapore today but the island was once covered with them. Nutmeg plantations used to clad the area around Orchard Road, Scotts Road and Mount Elizabeth. Captain William Scott, the son of the British explorer James Scott, was a nutmeg and cocoa plantation owner here and Scotts Road was named after him. Four million nuts were produced in 1848, but soon afterwards the plantations were devastated by pests and most dwindled into small plots as the land was sold off to property developers. Today, when towering skyscrapers, shopping malls and offices line these streets, it is hard to imagine that the area was once infested with tigers and that wealthy merchants with their retinues of servants used to stroll here in the cool shade of the nutmeg trees.

• *THAI*

Yhingthai Palace

No-frills, genuine Thai cuisine is served at this restaurant.
⊠ *36 Purvis Street,*
☎ *(65) 6337 1161.*

Naam

Offers delicious Thai dishes, especially their Tom Yam Soup.
⊠ *#02–22, Plaza Singapura, 68 Orchard Road,*
☎ *(65) 6339 9803.*

• *WESTERN*

Lawry's The Prime Rib

Specialities: Prime Rib and Yorkshire pudding.
⊠ *#02–30, Paragon, 290 Orchard Road,*
☎ *(65) 6836 3333.*

Original Sin

Mediterranean vegetarian cuisine.
⊠ *43, Jalan Merah Saga, Holland Village,*
☎ *(65) 6475 5605.*

Sol Spanish Restaurant

Authentic Spanish cuisine; good tapas menu, delicious sangria.
⊠ *Goodwood Park Hotel, 22 Scotts Road,*
☎ *(65) 6735 5322.*

Blue Lobster

Fresh seafood by the Singapore River.
⊠ *The Riverwalk, #b1–49/50,*
☎ *(65) 6538 0766.*

Ristorante Teatro

Fine cuisine with views of the gardens.
⊠ *Esplanade-Theatres on the Bay, #0114/16,*
☎ *(65) 6532 1922.*

Au Jardin

French cuisine with views of the gardens.
⊠ *Singapore Botanic Gardens Visitor Centre, 1 Cluny Road,*
☎ *(65) 6466 8812.*

• *JAPANESE*

Inagiku

Impeccable service, exquisite Japanese cuisine made from the freshest ingredients. The fresh sashimi is especially excellent.
⊠ *Raffles The Plaza, 2, Stamford Road,*
☎ *(65) 6338 8585.*

Ichiban Boshi

Authentic Japanese cuisine at reasonable prices. The central sushi conveyor belt is surrounded by private booths with elegant slatted dividers.

✉ #0213, Esplanade-Theatres on the Bay,
☎ (65) 6423 1151.

Wasabi Bistro

Japanese cuisine with distinct Californian influences.

✉ 4/F The Oriental, Marina Square,
☎ (65) 6885 3091.

• INTERNATIONAL

Mezza9

Japanese, Italian and Chinese food, and a martini bar.

✉ Grand Hyatt, 10-12 Scotts Road,
☎ (65) 6416 7189.

Blu

Enjoy fine Californian cuisine, served in an ambience of magnificent night-time city views and live jazz.

✉ Shangri-La Hotel, 22 Orange Grove Road,
☎ (65) 6730 2598.

The Cliff

Contempory seafood. Very popular in Singapore, especially on Sundays, and offered by all the major hotels.

✉ The Sentosa, 2 Bukit Manis Road, Sentosa,
☎ (65) 6371 1425.

Baden Baden

German food is a speciality at this restaurant.

✉ 42 Lorong Mambong, Holland Village,
☎ (65) 6468 5585.

Pierside Kitchen & Bar

Seafood.

✉ One Fullerton, #01-01,
☎ (65) 6438 0400.

Above: Intriguing foodstuffs line the five-foot way in front of this Chinatown shop.

Bean Curd

Bean curd is eaten as an alternative to meat by many health-watchers and vegetarians as it has twice as much protein weight for weight, minus the fat. It dates back 2000 years to the Han Dynasty when it was invented by a Taoist prince. It is made from soya beans which are processed by soaking, grinding, boiling and coagulating into a jelly-like ivory curd. Its versatility makes it a favourite ingredient among Chinese chefs, who have mastered the art of cooking the curd to emulate the texture and appearance of meat. It is delicious in any shape or form, be it as drink, stir-fry, in soup or steamed.

Below: *Hawker stalls outside the ornate Lau Pa Sat Festival Market.*

• HAWKER CENTRES
Hawkers Alley
Street dining at its best can be found at this hawker centre.
⊠ *Clarke Quay, River Valley Rd.*

Bugis Street
Malay, Indonesian, Thai and Chinese food. Evenings are particularly busy, when passers-by are accosted by touts brandishing menus.
⊠ *Bugis Village.*

Cuppage Centre
A food court in the basement, with the usual noodle, chicken rice and claypot outlets, as well as a drink and dessert stall.

⊠ *55 Cuppage Rd, off Orchard Rd.*

Chinatown Complex Hawker Centre
A wide range of dishes can be obtained here, especially Chinese cuisine.
⊠ *Block 335, 1st Floor, Smith St.*

The South and West
Alkaff Mansion
Enjoy an Indonesian buffet or western (mainly French) cuisine.
⊠ *10 Telok Blangah Green (Mt Faber),*
☎ *(65) 6278 6979.*

Au Petit Salut
Country French cuisine is served at this restaurant.
⊠ *Lorong Merah Saga, Holland Village,*
☎ *(65) 6475 1976.*

Ponggol Seafood Restaurant
Delicious selection of seafood specials.
⊠ *World Trade Centre,*
☎ *(65) 6448 8511.*

Restaurants

Raffles Marina Yacht Club

The restaurant serves both western and local food. Open to non-members on weekdays only.
✉ 10 Tuas West,
☎ (65) 6861 8000.

The North

Ramu's Curry

Delicious southern Indian cuisine is served here.
✉ Thomson Rd.

West Lake

Good Chinese food.
✉ Farrer Road.

The East

The Mango Tree

Indian food with a view of the coast.
✉ 1000 East Coast Parkway, B23,
☎ (65) 6442 8655,
✆ the_mangotree@ckrk.fwsl.com

East Coast Lagoon Food Center

A variety of hawker fare available here; there is something for everyone.
✉ along East Coast Parkway.

The Beach Hut

Alfresco buffet, particularly good on Sunday mornings.
✉ 1000 East Coast Parkway (close to McDonalds).

Cheng Heng Eating House

A good place to try Peranakan food.
✉ 220 East Coast Road,
☎ (65) 6344 6813.

Sentosa

Apart from food outlets at some of the tourist attractions, such as those at Underwater World, the Rasa Sentosa food centre near the ferry terminal and at the hotels, there is also a Mississippi-style riverboat restaurant in Sentosa. Here visitors can enjoy Chinese cuisine on the upper deck and fast food on the lower deck, while the bridge deck offers diners a scenic view of the Singapore skyline. This is a dining experience not to be missed.

An Aromatic Past
'Serai' is the local name for lemon grass, a characteristic ingredient of Southeast Asian cooking, and Geylang Serai was once the site of a lemon grass plantation. Mills in the area processed the crop to produce citronella, the fragrant essential oil used in perfumery.

Fishy Business
According to a 1992 report, the total annual supply of fresh fish, farm-bred or caught locally, amounted to 11,547 tonnes. Local fishermen use three main methods: trawling, gill-netting and long-lining. There are wholesale markets at Jurong and Punggol; the Jurong Fish Market also serves as a docking and bunkering base for foreign fishing vessels operating in this region. Factories nearby provide fish processing, ice-making and cold storage services. In Changi, the Marine Aquaculture Section researches and advises on farm management and fish husbandry. Ornamental fish exported in 1992 were worth S$70.5 million.

Pulau Ubin
Ubin Seafood
This popular restaurant is credited with having the best seafood cuisine in Singapore.
✉ *42 Pulau Ubin, Singapore 1750,*
☎ *(65) 6543 2489,*
🖱 *ubinseafood@ yahoo.com.sg*

Melaka
Restoran Peranakan Town House
There is a cultural show nightly (except Saturdays).
✉ *107 Jl Tun Tan Cheng Lock.*

Ole Sayang Restaurant
Authentic Peranakan cuisine is served at this family business; hospitable owners.
✉ *198 & 199 Taman Melaka Jaya,*
☎ *+606 283 1966.*

My Baba's
A good place for Nyonya cuisine.
✉ *164 Jl Munshi Abdullah,*
☎ *+606 284 3384.*

Gluttons' Corner at Jl Taman
Stalls here sell various Chinese, Malay and Indian dishes.
✉ *Bandar Hilir.*

Kuala Lumpur
There are food courts in most of the shopping centres in Kuala Lumpur. Bangsar, once a quiet suburb, is now a trendy area, with hawker stalls and restaurants offering all cuisines. Hotels have Chinese or western food, while coffee houses offer local and international fare.

• CHINESE
The Museum, The Legend Hotel
This restaurant is known particularly for its dim sum. It also has a wide selection of wines from all over.
✉ *100 Jalan Putra,*
☎ *+603 442 9888.*

Golden Phoenix Hotel
Cantonese specialities, fresh seafood and double-boiled soups.

✉ *Equatorial Kuala Lumpar, Jalan Sultan Ismail,*
☎ *+603 261 7777.*

Seasons View Chinese Restaurant, Grand Seasons Hotel
Try the steamboat (hot pot) or braised shark's fin soup with fresh scallops.
✉ *72 Jalan Pahang,*
☎ *+603 297 8888 ext. 8828.*

• MALAY
Alexis
For the casual diner, Alexis serves Italian (try the lasagne) as well as Malaysian and Singaporean. Head for the desserts for a fulfilling visit.
✉ *29 Jalan Telawi, 3 Bangsar Baru,*
☎ *+603 284 2880.*

Rasa Utara Restaurant
Authentic Malay cuisine in the heart of the shopping district.
✉ *BS003, Basement 1, BB Plaza Jalan Bukit Bintan,*
☎ *+603 241 9246.*

• INDIAN

Seetharam Family Curry House

A selection of South Indian sweetmeats, banana leaf rice, *thosai* (flour pancakes), and nasi lemak (rice cooked in coconut milk.

☒ *237 Jalan Tun Sambanthan Brickfields,*

☎ *+603 2274 6722.*

Annalakshmi

Possibly the most renowned vegetarian North and South Indian restaurant in KL. Has dishes without garlic or onions.

☒ *44-46, Jalan Maarof, Bangsar Baru,*

☎ *+603 282 3799.*

The Taj

This restaurant specializes in Northern Indian cuisine and is a three-time award winner of Best Indian Restaurant by the Malaysian Tourism Board. You can't go wrong here.

☒ *Crown Princess Hotel City Square Centre, Jalan Tun Razak,*

☎ *+603 262 5522.*

• INTERNATIONAL

O'Las Western Restaurant

Steak and kebabs – definitely one for meat lovers.

☒ *Grand Seasons Hotel, 72 Jalan Pahang,*

☎ *+603 297 8888.*

Müller's Sausage Haus

Bratwurst to Käsewurst, and a selection of German beer.

☒ *241-1 Jalan Ampang,*

☎ *+603 244 4167.*

Grappa Soho

Italian restaurant serving crispy pizzas and tiramisu.

☒ *First Floor Wisma Peladang, 2 Jalan Bukit Bintang,*

☎ *+603 245 0080.*

Buddha Jumps Over the Wall

Many of the shops in Chinatown specialize in Chinese herbs and medicines, and also in culinary delicacies. The treasures of the sea (see panel, page 66) attain their ultimate grandeur in an exquisite, not to mention expensive, dish called Buddha Jumps Over the Wall, an extravagant broth of abalone, highest quality shark's fin, scallops, fish maw, sea cucumber and Chinese mushrooms, fit for an emperor.

Below: *Spicy Nyonya food is served in this restaurant in Peranakan Place.*

Above: *Eating out in New Bugis Street, a pale imitation of the old centre of Singapore's nightlife which was demolished to make way for the MRT.*
Opposite: *Elaborate costumes and make-up, dramatic music and movement make Chinese street Opera a spectacular entertainment.*

Lucky Numbers
Betting on horses and entering lotteries are the only legal forms of **gambling** in Singapore, and Singaporeans spend about $1 billion on lottery tickets each year. They are great believers in lucky numbers and tend to crowd around after a car crash, not ghoulishly to peer at the victims, but to note down the cars' registration numbers for future use.

ENTERTAINMENT
Nightlife

Singapore really comes alive when night falls, with entertainment galore to amuse even the most discerning of visitors. The city boasts a plethora of interesting night spots, ranging from discos, jazz clubs, karaoke bars and pubs to various theatres, cinemas and cultural shows.

For the young-at-heart there are many **nightclubs** and **discos** to choose from. For a pulsating atmosphere and ear-splittingly loud music, head for Zouk, Top Ten, Centro, The Liquid Room or the Hard Rock Café (see page 77). **Jazz** lovers can visit Harry's Bar (see page 77) and Jazz@Southbridge at Boat Quay, and Somerset's Bar at Swissôtel The Stamford (see page 56).

For a uniquely Singaporean **cabaret act**, try the Boom Boom Room at Far East Square. The show starts at 23:00 with a non-stop routine of 'stand-ups' starring Kumar, the drag queen local television personality whose repertoire is extremely risqué and told in 'Singlish' – the local hybrid English language. If you do not wish to be dragged on stage to participate – the jokes will be at your expense – you'd do best to avoid the front seats.

At **Clarke Quay** there is a host of pubs, restaurants and discos, including Crazy Elephant (*see* page 77).

For **indigenous cultural shows**, spend an evening at the Meritus Mandarin Hotel (*see* page 57) or the Singa Inn Seafood Restaurant. There are nightly performances of the lion dance and other Chinese, Malay and Indian dances from Singapore and its Southeast Asian neighbours.

During the Festival of the Hungry Ghosts in August and September, and for other festivals and temple celebrations, Chinese operas (*see* below) are frequently performed. For details of these performances, contact the Singapore Tourist Information Service (*see* page 84).

Music

Chinese Opera

Chinese opera, or *wayang*, is often performed at street corners on makeshift stages during festivals such as Yu Lan Jie, the Festival of the Hungry Ghosts, Chinese New Year or clan birthdays. The actors, lavishly plastered with layers of make-up and liberally rouged, are dressed in splendid, colourful costumes of embroidered brocade, and are decked with flags and elaborate headgear.

The stories are quite easy to follow as the drama unfolds and the heroes and villains make their exaggerated movements accompanied by live music. The stories are based on

Jazz@Southbridge
✉ 82B Boat Quay
☎ (65) 6327 4671/2
🖥 www.southbridge jazz.com.sg
M Raffles Place

Boom Boom Room
✉ Far East Square
☎ (65) 6435 0030
📧 info@boomboom room.com.sg
🖥 www.boomboom room.com.sg
M Raffles Place

Singa Inn Seafood Restaurant
✉ 920 East Coast Parkway, Singapore 449875
☎ (65) 6345 1111

Esplanade-Theatres on the Bay
✉ 1 Esplanade Drive,
☎ (65) 6828 8222,
🖥 www.esplanade.com
🚌 SBS36, 57, 75, 77, 97, 106, 111, 133, 162, 171, 195, 700A, 857, 960/1
M City Hall
🕐 10:00–22:00hrs (or half an hour after the last performance)

Victoria Concert Hall
✉ 11 Empress Place,
☎ (65) 6338 1239 or 6338 1230

Victoria Theatre
✉ 9 Empress Place,
☎ (65) 6338 8283
📠 (65) 6339 5440

Substation
✉ 45 Armenian Street,
☎ (65) 6337 7800,
🖳 www.substation.org.sg

Black Box (of TheatreWorks)
✉ Fort Canning Centre, Cox Terrace,
☎ (65) 6338 8297,
📠 (65) 6338 4077,
📧 tworks@singnet.com.sg
🖳 www.theatreworks.org.sg
Ⓜ Dhoby Ghaut

Singapore Indoor Stadium
✉ 2 Stadium Walk,
☎ (65) 6344 2660,
📠 (65) 6344 5903,
🖳 www.sis.gov.sg

ancient Chinese epics dealing with love, treachery and war and inevitably end with the triumph of good over evil.

The Singapore Symphony Orchestra
Established in 1979, the SSO is Singapore's only professional orchestra. Under the direction of its resident conductor, Lan Shui, it gives regular concerts of music from the Baroque to the 20th century at the **Esplanade-Theatres On The Bay** and at various open-air venues. It has accompanied many distinguished soloists including Luciano Pavarotti and Placido Domingo.

Theatre

Theatre in Singapore is cosmopolitan, and various venues like the **Victoria Theatre** in Empress Place, the **Substation** in Armenian Street, the **Black Box (of TheatreWorks)** in Canning Park, **Singapore Indoor Stadium** and **Esplanade-Theatres On The Bay** (*see* page 29 and panel, page 71) stage a variety of local as well as international productions of plays, musicals and ballets. Details of performances at these venues can be obtained from local newspapers or from the individual venues themselves.

Cinema

Singapore has over 50 cinemas, and new films arrive here very quickly. Details are listed in the daily press. All cinemas are air-conditioned.

Festivals

Every ethnic group in Singapore has its own festivals, mostly related to its religion. Almost every month of the year sees a celebration of some form or other, bringing a visual feast of colour, pomp and ceremony

which is enjoyed by the whole population. In a peaceful and harmonious society, Singaporeans respect and celebrate one another's festivals with relish.

Chinese Festivals

The most vibrant and colourful festival in the Chinese calendar is the **Lunar New Year**, when the whole of Chinatown is ablaze with lights from ceremonial red lanterns, and the streets are bedecked with traditional decorations mainly in red, the colour of good luck. The Singapore River is the venue for colourful stalls selling food, handicrafts and New Year souvenirs to bring luck. The celebration starts with family reunion dinner on New Year's Eve, followed by open-house over the next few days. It is a time for forgiveness and for settling old debts. The festival lasts for 15 days and concludes with a big celebration called **Chap Goh Mei**.

The seventh month of the lunar year is devoted to the **Festival of the Hungry Ghosts**, during which the gates of hell are thrown open and the spirits of the dead are released on 'parole' to roam the earth. Food, prayers, incense and 'hell money' are

Above: Chinatown blazes with red and gold, the colours of good luck, for the Lunar New Year celebrations.
Opposite: Orchestral music being performed in Victoria Concert Hall.

Tying the Knot
In 1995, **Chap Goh Mei**, the last day of the Lunar New Year celebrations, happened to fall on 14 February – St Valentine's Day. The multicultural Singaporeans rushed to take advantage of the coincidence: over 1000 couples were married on this doubly auspicious day.

Above: *Huge joss-sticks are burned for the Festival of the Hungry Ghosts.*
Opposite: *During the Hindu festival of Thaipusam, extra-ordinary acts of religious devotion are undergone when tranced penitents pierce their flesh with skewers and hooks supporting heavy* kavadis *decorated with peacock feathers and flowers.*

Festival Calendar
Jan • New Year's Day (Orchard Rd); Ponggal: Tamil Harvest Festival (Perumal Temple, Serangoon Rd)
Jan–Feb • Thaipusam (Perumal Temple); Chinese Lunar New Year (Chinatown); Chingay (Orchard Rd); Ramadan; Hari Raya Puasa

---

offered to appease the spirits. Celebratory dinners are held as well as performances of Chinese street operas or *wayang* (*see* page 71). No marriages or betrothals will be conducted during this month, or dangerous journeys, such as sea voyages, embarked on.

The **Moon Cake** or **Mid-Autumn Festival** commemorates the patriot Zhu Yuan Zhang, who plotted to overthrow the tyrannical rule of the Yuan dynasty in the 14th century, and is said to have passed his plans to his fellow rebels hidden in mooncakes. Hence today, these moon-shaped pastries with sweet fillings of red bean and lotus seed paste are exchanged as gifts. Lanterns were also used to send signals during the rebellion, so lanterns of all shapes and sizes are carried in processions. In Singapore the Chinese Garden is the special venue for this most beautiful of all the Chinese festivals.

Islamic Festivals

In the Muslim community **Hari Raya Puasa** marks the end of the fasting month of Ramadan. The festival begins with morning prayers in the mosque, followed by a thanksgiving feast. It is a time for forgiveness and a strengthening of bonds in the community. New clothes are donned, houses decorated and friends of all races are invited to share this joyous occasion. The Malay area of Geylang is illuminated to welcome the festive season.

Hari Raya Haji is the celebration of the conclusion of the Haj pilgrimage to Mecca, at which pilgrims are given the title of Haji (for men) or Hajjah (for women). Goats or buffaloes are sacrificed and the meat distributed to the poor.

Indian Festivals

Deepavali celebrates the victory of good over evil, symbolized by the legendary slaying of the oppressive Narakasura by Lord Krishna. It marks the beginning of the Indian New Year, and for the business community it is a time for settling debts. It is also believed that the souls of departed relatives descend to earth during this festival, and oil lamps are lit to guide them. Like the New Year festivals of the Chinese and Muslims, it is celebrated with 'open-house' visits among friends of all races. Little India's temples and streets are decorated with spectacular displays of lights, tinsel and garlands.

The most dramatic Indian festival is **Thaipusam**, when devotees go through a strict and careful spiritual preparation before embarking on a ritual journey of penitential self-mutilation. They pierce their bodies with metal hooks supporting heavy structures called

> **Festival Calendar**
> **Feb–Mar** • Birthday of the Monkey God (Monkey God Temple, Eng Hoon St)
> **Mar–Apr** • Qing Ming; Good Friday (procession from St Joseph's, Victoria St)
> **May–Jun** • Vesak Day (Buddhist festival); Hari Raya Haji (celebration of pilgrimage to Mecca); Dragon Boat Races (Marina Bay)
> **9 Aug** • National Day
> **Aug–Sep** • Festival of the Hungry Ghosts; Mooncake Festival (Chinese Gardens)
> **Sep–Oct** • Birthday of the Monkey God; Navarathiri (Sri Thandayuthapani Temple, Tank Rd)
> **Oct–Nov** • Festival of Nine Emperor Gods (Kiu Ong Yiah Temple, Serangoon Rd); Pilgrimage to Kusu Island
> **Nov** • Thimithi (Firewalking festival, Sri Mariamman Temple, South Bridge Rd); Deepavali
> **Dec** • Christmas

Above: *Singapore really comes alive when night falls.*

kavadis; these are decorated with peacock feathers and offerings. In their tranced state, not a drop of blood is shed as they make their way from the Sri Srinivasa Perumal Temple in Serangoon Road to the Sri Thandayuthapani Temple in Tank Road.

Another spectacular festival is **Thimithi**, the fire-walking ceremony, held at the Sri Mariamman Temple in South Bridge Road. Devotees defy all sense of pain by walking across a bed of burning coals without so much as a flinch or a blister to show for their ordeal.

Vesak

The festival celebrated with great ceremonial ritual by Buddhists is **Vesak Day**, which commemorates the birth and enlightenment of Buddha and his entry into Nirvana.

The day starts with chanting of the sutras by saffron-clad monks, while devotees visit the temples to pray and meditate and to make offerings. Acts of generosity known as *dana* are observed by Buddhist organizations and temples. These include the freeing of caged birds and animals, visiting and giving alms to the poor and needy, while some Buddhist youths organize mass blood donation at hospitals. The celebration concludes with a candlelit procession through the streets. Observers as well as devotees are welcome to join in the celebration at Buddhist temples.

Chingay Singapore

Participants from around the world take part in this parade. Chingay means 'the art of masquerading' and was once a purely Chinese procession, but Singapore's other cultural groups joined in. Nowadays it is a glamorous showcase of cultures from countries like the USA, UK, New Zealand, Malaysia, Japan, the Philippines, Taiwan, Seychelles and many more. It is held annually on the first Saturday of the Lunar New Year celebrations in Orchard Road, in the heart of the shopping and entertainment district. It attracts over 100,000 spectators, both locals and tourists, and is shown live on Singapore Television.

NIGHTCLUBS, BARS & DISCOS

Nightclubs, Bars and Discos

Centro

This was voted the best nightspot of the year 2002.

⊠ One Fullerton,
☎ (65) 6220 2288.

Fabulous Fizz

Champagne bar.

⊠ Esplanade-Theatres on the Bay,
☎ (65) 6336 9918.

Maracas Cocina Latina

Latin bar, featuring Latin-inspired cocktails and Mexican food.

⊠ 30 Victoria Street, Chijmes,
☎ (65) 6336 9151,
📱 (65) 6883 1507.

The Long Bar

This is the best place to savour the Singapore Sling.

⊠ Raffles Hotel, 1 Beach Road,
☎ (65) 6337 1886.

Crazy Elephant

Unpretentious and relaxing; dance to Rock 'n' Roll and the Blues.

⊠ Clarke Quay,
☎ (65) 6337 1990.

Carnegie's

This dance club and pub is rowdy and crowded and makes for an entertaining night out.

⊠ Far East Square,
☎ (65) 6534 0850.

Wala Wala

Laid-back neighbourhood bar.

⊠ 31 Lorong Mambong,
☎ (65) 6432 4288.

Bar Sá Vanh

Indochinese bar with downtempo grooves.

⊠ 49A Club Street,
☎ (65) 6323 0145.

Zouk

An internationally renowned dance club in three warehouses joined together.

⊠ 17, Jiak Kim Road,
☎ (65) 6738 2988.

Harry's Bar

This is the place to go if you love jazz. Try the outlets at Boat Quay and Esplanade-Theatres on the Bay.

⊠ 28 Boat Quay,
☎ (65) 6538 3029; or
⊠ 8 Raffles Avenue,
#01-05/07 Esplanade Mall, ☎ (65) 6334 0132, ⊠ www.harrys-bar.com.sg

Ice Cold Beer

In an old shophouse, this beer bar is casual and relaxed.

⊠ 9 Emerald Hill,
☎ (65) 6735 9929.

Top Ten

A bit sleazy, but a very popular place.

⊠ 400 Orchard Road, #04–35/36 Orchard Towers, Singapore 238875,
☎ (65) 732 3077/8

The Liquid Room

This was one of the first dance clubs in Singapore to offer techno, trance, and house music.

⊠ Robertson Quay,
☎ (65) 6333 8117,
🖥 www.liquidroom.com.sg

Hard Rock Café

Part of the international chain.

⊠ 50 Cuscaden Road,
☎ (65) 6235 5232,
🖥 www.hardrock.com.sg

Above: *The style and elegance of a bygone age of travel are recreated in the opulent dining saloon of the E & O Express.*

EXCURSIONS

Singapore is pivotally placed for excursions to its neighbouring countries: across the causeway to mainland **Malaysia** and over the sea to **Indonesia**. A short flight or boat trip will whisk you to island resorts like the legendary Pulau Tioman, the ultra-chic Pangkor Laut Resort or to Johor, the 'backyard' of Singapore. A trip on the Eastern and Oriental train (E & O) will take you in style to Kuala Lumpur, capital of Malaysia. The islands of Batam and Bintan in the Riau Archipelago in Indonesia offer tempting rustic scenery as well as sea and sand.

Johor

Linked by a 1km (half-mile) causeway to Singapore is Johor, the southernmost state in Peninsular Malaysia. Every weekend the causeway is congested with traffic from Singapore as crowds cross to patronize the inexpensive (compared with Singapore) seafood restaurants in Johor Bahru or Kukup while others head for the beach in Desaru.

Johor Bahru, the capital of Johor, is a bustling town where modernity mingles with the colonial past. Its appeal lies in its shopping complexes, seafood restaurants and grand buildings of a bygone era. Places worth visiting are the **Istana Besar** (Grand Palace), the **Royal Abu Bakar Museum** and the **Istana Bukit Serene**, the official residence of the present sultan (only the garden is open to the public). The **Sultan Abu Bakar Mosque** is nearby.

Johor
Location: Map A–C4
Distance from Singapore: 20km
(12 miles)

Istana Besar
✉ Kawasan Kebun Bunga, Johor Bahru
☎ +60 7 223 4935;
224 9960 (Tourist Department of Johor)
🕙 07:00–19:00 daily

Royal Abu Bakar Museum
✉ Johor Grand Palace
☎ +60 7 223 0555
📠 +60 7 224 8476
🕙 09:00–17:00 Sat–Thu
(last admission 16:00)

JOHOR & MELAKA

Southwest of Johor Bahru is **Kukup**, a fishing village raised on stilts. Here the seafood restaurants are renowned for their prawn and chilli crab dishes. It is for these culinary delights that tourists and Singaporeans flock here, especially at weekends.

On the northeast coast is **Desaru**, Johor's mainland beach resort (it also has a marine park of seven islands with fine beaches just off the coast). Desaru's 20km (13 miles) of sandy beaches offer a convenient respite from city life for Singaporeans. Some 88km (55 miles) from Johor Bahru, Desaru is accessible by car, bus or ferry from Singapore.

Melaka

The historic town of Melaka was founded by Parameswara, a refugee Sumatran prince, in the late 14th century. It became the centre of the Malay Sultanate during the 15th century. Its importance as a spice trading post brought it to the attention of the Portuguese, who conquered the port in 1511. The **Porta de Santiago**, the gateway which is all that remains of the huge fortress of **A Famosa**, is now the only concrete legacy of Portuguese rule. The Dutch defeated the Portuguese in 1641, colonizing Melaka until it was taken over by the British in 1824.

The influence of its European rulers over the centuries, in addition to the Peranakan and Malay cultures, have given the town a cultural richness. Its famous Peranakan (Nyonya) cuisine, a blend

Melaka
Location: Map A–B3
Distance from Singapore: 245km (152 miles)

Stadthuys
⊠ Dutch Square
🕘 09:00–18:00 Mon, Wed–Sun; closed Fri 12:15–14:45
💰 RM2

St Paul's Church
⊠ Bukit St Paul
☎ +60 6 282 0685 (Tourist Information Centre)
🕘 09:00–17:00 Mon–Sat

Christ Church
⊠ Jalan Gereja
☎ +60 6 283 6538
🕘 09:00–17:00 Mon–Sat

Below: *The historic colonial Stadthuys and Christ Church in Melaka.*

Kuala Lumpur
Location: Map A–A3
Distance from
Singapore: 390km
(242 miles)

Sultan Abdul Samad
Building
✉ Jalan Raja
☎ +60 3 2696 6135
📠 +60 3 2694 8796
🕐 08:00–16:45 Mon–
Fri, 08:00–13:00 Sat

St Mary's Church
✉ Jalan Raja
☎ +60 3 2694 5470
🕐 08:00–18:00 daily

Masjid Jamek
✉ Jalan Tun Perak
☎ +60 3 2274 6063
or +60 3 2693 6664

of Malay and Chinese culinary styles, is a must for food lovers. The heritage trail around old Peranakan shophouses, antique shops and Chinese temples, and colonial buildings such as the ruined **St Paul's Church**, the Dutch **Stadthuys** of 1650 (now the museum) and the 18th-century **Christ Church** will keep visitors enthralled. It is worth staying in Melaka for a night or two.

Kuala Lumpur

Merdeka Square is a good starting point for your tour of Kuala Lumpur, or KL as it is known locally. In colonial days the square was the city's sports ground. The handsome **Sultan Abdul Samad Building**, **St Mary's Church**, **Masjid Jamek** at the birthplace of KL at the confluence of the Gombak and Klang Rivers, and **Infokraf**, the craft centre, are all within walking distance of the square.

Below: *KL's Moorish-style Sultan Abdul Samad Building.*

Across the Klang River is the **Central Market (Pasar Seni)**, an Aladdin's cave of

shops and stalls selling arts, crafts, food and artefacts from Malaysia and its neighbouring countries. Nearby in Jalan Petaling is **Chinatown**, a hive of busy market stalls selling fake designer goods, clothes, electronic equipment and other goods at bargain prices. The old shophouses flanking the street markets are showcases of the age-old Chinese lifestyle, with traditional medicine shops, coffee shops, ironmongers and goldsmiths. The groceries offer curious-looking edibles like wind-dried ducks (which look as if they have been flattened by a steamroller), dried mushrooms and sea cucumbers, while Chinese sausages hang in festoons from hooks in the five-foot way.

The **Lake Gardens**, the green lung of the city, comprise 92ha (230 acres) of beautiful vegetation, with an **Orchid Garden**, **Bird Park** and a **Butterfly Park**. The **National Museum**, near the Lake Gardens, is worth a visit too. It has extensive exhibitions of arts and crafts, local history, native flora and fauna, weapons and currency, in addition to a display of vintage transport in the grounds.

KL is renowned for its shopping, and can offer better bargains than Singapore. The main shopping centres are dotted around the streets of the **Golden Triangle**: Jalan Bukit Bintang, Jalan Sultan Ismail and Jalan Imbi. There are other large departmental stores at Jalan Ampang and Jalan Tun Razak, and the more traditional shophouses along Jalan Tuanku Abdul Rahman.

Pulau Pangkor Laut

This little island is one of the most exclusive resorts in Malaysia. The luxurious **Pangkor Laut Resort** has villa-style accommodation centred on **Royal Bay**, the main beach front, and **Coral Bay** in the next cove. The villas are fashioned in the style of traditional Malay houses built on stilts, some over the sea while others perch dramatically on the cliff.

The jungle-clad interior harbours bountiful wildlife, including hornbills and long-tailed macaques. The magnificent **Emerald Bay**, on the opposite side of the island away from the villas, has been voted one of the best 100 beaches in the world.

Above: *A villa overlooking Royal Bay on luxurious Pulau Pangkor Laut.*

Central Market, KL
⊠ Jalan Hang Kasturi (within walking distance of the Putraline LRT's Pasar Seni station)
☎ +60 3 2274 9966
℡ +60 3 2274 9906
🖥 www.centralmarket.com.my
🕘 10:00–22:00 daily

Lake Gardens, KL
⊠ between Jalan Persiaran Mahameru and Jalan Kebun Bunga
☎ +60 3 2691 6011
🕘 09:00–18:00 daily

Pulau Pangkor Laut
Location: Map A–A2
Distance from Singapore: 570km (354 miles)

Pangkor Laut Resort
☎ +60 3 2145 9000
🖥 www.pangkorlautresort.com

Pulau Tioman

This island was chosen as the location for 'Bali Hai' in the film version of *South Pacific* in the 1950s. Its rugged forested terrain is fringed with golden sands bathed by warm clear waters. Tioman is a favourite with scuba divers and snorkellers, as the rich coral reef harbours some of the most diverse marine life in Malaysia, notably in the water off **Salang Beach**. The island is dominated by the **Berjaya Tioman Beach, Golf and Spa Resort**, the only international-standard luxury hotel here. There is plenty of more modest accommodation in chalets, A-frame huts and beach bungalows. Malay villages dotted around the island can be reached along jungle paths or by sea bus.

Pulau Tioman
Location: Map A–C3
Distance from
Singapore: 190km
(118 miles)

Berjaya Tioman Beach,
Golf and Spa Resort
✉ P.O.Box 4, Mersing,
86807 Johor, Malaysia
☎ +60 9 419 1000
✆ +60 9 419 1718
🖳 reserv@b-tioman.com
💻 www.
berjayaresorts.com/

The Indonesian Islands

Scattered across the South China Sea southeast of Singapore is a cluster of some 3000 Indonesian islands – the **Riau Archipelago**.

Bintan, the largest island, is relatively undeveloped. Most of the population is concentrated in **Tanjung Pinang**, the quaint main town with its bustling port. Water taxis, known as *pompong*, can be hired to travel round the coast of Bintan or to visit neighbouring islands. **Senggarang**, a rustic fishing village just north of Tanjung Pinang, has a large population of Teochew Chinese who live in **Kampong Cina** (Chinese Village) in stilted houses perched over the sea.

Bintan's main attraction lies in its long stretch of palm-fringed sandy beaches on the northern coast, accessible from the south only along dirt tracks or by boat.

Bintan Island
Location: Map A–C4
Distance from
Singapore: 35km
(22 miles)

Mayang Sari Beach
Resort
☎ (62) 778 323 088
💻 www.
nirwanagardens.com

Banyan Tree Bintan
☎ (62) 770 693 100
💻 www.
banyantree.com

The **Mayang Sari Beach Resort**, with 100 beach chalets, offers cosy accommodation. There is a coffee house with indoor and outdoor dining. Next to the resort is the Mana Mana Beach Club, with windsurfing, scuba diving, snorkelling, sailing, waterskiing and jetskiing. There are restaurants, bars and a pro-shop, but no accommodation. The **Banyan Tree Bintan** is a luxury resort with villas perched high on a cliff, a poolside restaurant and bar. An 18-hole golf course, pool, tennis court and water sports are available to guests. For dining, the Kelong Restaurant, built on stilts stretching out into the sea, serves fresh seafood. Live fish and shellfish are kept in netted pontoons accessed by walkways and are fished out as they are chosen from the menu.

Duty-free **Batam Island** is largely undeveloped, with rustic Malay villages hugging the sea edge while pockets of settlement are scattered on the island. Nagoya, the main town, has good seafood restaurants, built in *kelong* style above the sea. Two of the island's major resorts are the **Batam View Beach Resort** and the **Turi Beach Resort**. Batam View, on a peninsula surrounded by turquoise water, offers various water sports, a 36-hole golf course and a seafood restaurant. The Balinese-style Turi Beach Resort has all the amenities of an international hotel with a health club and water sports. There are regular Indonesian cultural shows as well as weekend seafood barbecues at the poolside.

Batam Island
Location: Map A–C4
Distance from Singapore: 75km (47 miles)

Batam View Beach Resort
New Century Tours Corporation (Pte Ltd) in Singapore:
☎ (65) 6846 3255
📠 (65) 6746 7897
🖥 www.batamviewresort.com/

Turi Beach Resort
✉ Jl Hong Lekui, Nongsa
☎ (62) 778 761 080
📠 (62) 778 761 043
🖥 www.holidaybagus.com/Batam_TuriBeach_FS.htm

Opposite: *Clear blue water laps the coast of Pulau Tioman, one of the world's loveliest islands.*
Below: *The palm-fringed beach of Pasir Panjang runs all along the north coast of Bintan.*

Above: *A network of modern express-ways carries traffic all over the island.*

Crime and Punishment

Singapore has one of the lowest crime rates in the world and the government intends to keep it that way. Harsh punishments are meted out to offenders: the death penalty for drug trafficking and murder, the cane for lesser crimes. A case in point is the caning of the American teenager, Michael Fay in 1994, who was given four strokes of the rotan for vandalizing cars (reduced from six after the intervention of President Clinton). Singapore is wryly described as a 'fine city'. There are fines for any number of offences: littering, jay-walking, failure to flush public toilets, spitting in public places, smoking on public transport or in any public building.

Tourist Information

The Singapore Tourist Promotion Board has offices worldwide for general assistance and information.

Head office: ✉ Suntec City Mall, 3 Temasek Blvd. #01-35/37/39/41. North Bridge Road, Singapore 0617, ☎ 1800 332 5066, 📠 339 9423.

Information centres: ✉ Liang Court, 1/F Liang Court Shopping Centre, 177 River Valley Road, ☎ 6336 2888. ✉ Prinsep Place, 44 Prinsep Street, #01-01/02-01, ☎ 6336 3660. ✉ Bencoolen, #01-09, Sunshine Plaza, 91 Bencoolen Street, ☎ 1800 238 2388. ✉ Plaza Singapura, 1/F Plaza Singapura, 68 Orchard Road, ☎ 6332 9298.

Other STPB offices: Bombay, Chicago, Frankfurt, Hong Kong, London, Los Angeles, New York, Osaka, Paris, Perth, Seoul, Shanghai, Sydney, Taipei, Tokyo, Toronto, Zurich.

Entry Formalities

All visitors entering Singapore must be in possession of a valid passport or an inter-nationally recognized travel document.

Visa requirements: 1. Citizens of the fol-lowing countries do not need visas for social visits: Australia, Bangladesh, Brunei, Canada, Hong Kong, Liechtenstein, Malaysia, Monaco, Netherlands, New Zealand, Sri Lanka, Switzerland, the UK and the USA; holders of diplomatic, special or official pass-ports of the Philippines and Thailand.

2. Citizens of the fol-lowing countries do not need visas for stays of up to 3 months; visas are required for stays exceeding 3 months: Austria,

Belgium, Denmark, Finland, France, Germany, Italy, Iceland, Luxembourg, Japan, Norway, South Korea, Spain and Sweden.

3. Visas are required for the following nationals: Afghanistan, Algeria, Cambodia, India, Iraq, Jordan, Laos, Lebanon, Libya, Pakistan, People's Republic of China, CIS (Russia), Syria, Tunisia, Vietnam, Yemen, Hong Kong Documents of Identity issued in Hong Kong, and stateless persons residing in these countries.

4. Passport holders of the Russian Federation, People's Republic of China, Laos, Vietnam, Cambodia and Afghanistan may transit in Singapore for 36 hours without a visa, provided they hold confirmed onward/return airline tickets and onward facilities to their next destination.

5. No visas are needed for other nationalities not mentioned above for social visits not exceeding 14 days.

Holders of Taiwan passports do not need visas as tourists but must have visa cards, which are free from any Singapore overseas mission, the airlines or shipping companies.

Note: As regulations change from time to time, international visitors should check with the nearest Singapore overseas mission before departure. The final decision concerning entry into the country, irrespective of whether the person has a visa or not, is at the discretion of the Immigration Officer at the point of entry. Women in advanced states of pregnancy (six months or more) intending to visit Singapore should make prior applications to the nearest Singapore overseas mission or the Immigration Department.

Singapore Immigration and Checkpoint Authority,
✉ ICA Building,
10 Kallang Building,
☎ 6391 6100.

Health Requirements

No vaccinations are required for Singapore except cholera or yellow fever if you have come from or visited an endemic zone 6 days prior to arriving in the country.

TRAFFICKING, MANUFACTURING, IMPORTING AND EXPORTING OF ILLEGAL DRUGS SUCH AS OPIUM, HEROIN, CANNABIS, MORPHINE, COCAINE AND CANNABIS RESIN CARRY THE <u>DEATH PENALTY</u>.

Customs Formalities

Dutiable goods:
Liquors including wine, beer, ale, stout and port; tobacco, including cigarettes and cigars; garments and clothing accessories; leather handbags and wallets; imitation jewellery; chocolate and sugar confectionery; pastries, biscuits and cakes.

Non-dutiable goods:
Electronic and electri-

cal goods; cosmetics; cameras, clocks and watches; toys; jewellery, precious stones, precious metal; footwear; arts and crafts.

Duty-free concessions for visitors:

The following dutiable items may be brought into the country duty-free for personal consumption only: personal effects in reasonable quantities; prepared food such as chocolates, biscuits, cakes etc. not exceeding S$50.00 in value. Travellers above 18 years old, arriving from countries other than Malaysia and spending not less than 48 hours in Singapore, are entitled to a duty-free allowance of 1 litre spirits, 1 litre wine and 1 litre beer, stout, ale or port.

Prohibited items:

Controlled drugs and psychotropic substances; firecrackers; pistol- or revolver-shaped cigarette lighters; toy coins and toy currency notes; unauthorized repro-

ductions of copyright publications, records or cassettes, video tapes or discs; endangered species of wildlife and their by-products; obscene articles and publications; seditious and treasonable materials; chewing gum. Liquor, cigarettes and tobacco marked for export with the label 'Singapore Duty Not Paid' and cigarettes with the prefix 'E' are restricted to consumption outside Singapore. Re-importation is not permitted. For further clarification contact: The Customs Duty Officer, ✉ Duty Office Terminal 1, Singapore Changi Airport, Singapore 9181, ☎ 6542 7058, or The Customs Duty Officer, ✉ Duty Office Terminal 2, Singapore Changi Airport, Singapore 9181, ☎ 6543 0755.

Changi Airport

Airport tax: A S$15.00 Passenger Services Charge is payable at the airport on de-

parture. Coupons for the airport tax can be bought at most hotels, travel agencies and airline offices. Attach the coupon to your airline ticket.

Baggage storage: Both terminals provide baggage storage services at their arrival and departure halls.

Free tour: Passengers with at least four hours' transit time at Changi Airport can take a two-hour free tour of Singapore (The City Tour), run by the Civil Aviation Authority of Singapore, Singapore Airlines and STPB. To register, go to the 'Free City Sightseeing' desk in the transit lounge and show your boarding pass and passport. The guided tour gives you a taste of Singapore, passing through Chinatown, Little India, Lau Pa Sat Festival Market, the Colonial District and Merlion Park. Return with the coach to Changi Airport. The tour leaves at 10:30, 14:30 and 16:30 daily.

Medical Facilities

Singapore's medical facilities rank among the best in the world, with well-qualified doctors and dental surgeons. Pharmaceuticals are available from numerous outlets, including supermarkets, department stores, hotels and shopping centres. Registered pharmacists operate from 08:00 to 16:30. Travellers with medicine which may only be obtained on prescription under Singapore law, especially sleeping pills, antidepressants and stimulants, must have a prescription from a physician confirming that the medicine is to be used solely for the traveller's physical well-being. Most hotels have a doctor on call around the clock. Doctors are listed in the Yellow Pages of the Singapore phone book. Visitors could also consult doctors at the following hospitals:

Gleneagles Medical Centre, ✉ 6 Napier Road, Singapore 1025, ☎ 6470 3415.

Mount Alvernia Hospital, ✉ 820 Thomson Road, Singapore 2057, ☎ 6253 8023.

Mount Elizabeth Hospital, ✉ 3 Mount Elizabeth, Singapore 0922, ☎ 6737 2666.

Singapore General Hospital, ✉ Outram Road, Singapore 0316, ☎ 6222 3322.

Thomson Medical Centre, ✉ 339 Thomson Road, Singapore 1130, ☎ 6256 9494. As private medical fees are high in Singapore, visitors should ensure they are adequately covered by travel insurance.

Money Matters

You can change money at banks, hotels (usually at less favourable rates) and licensed money changers at most shopping complexes. It is not advisable to use unlicensed money dealers.

Currency: There is no restriction on the import or export of currency into or from

Singapore Airlines

The flag carrier of Singapore is one of the most successful airlines in the world and has won several awards in its existence of just over two decades. It had a modest beginning in May 1947, when Malayan Airways operated its first commercial flights linking Singapore, Kuala Lumpur, Ipoh and Penang. The airline was renamed Malaysian Airways in 1963 and later became Malaysia-Singapore Airlines (MSA). On 1 October 1972, it split into Malaysian Airline System (now Malaysia Airlines) and Singapore Airlines (SIA). Today, with its subsidiary SilkAir, it has a network connecting 87 cities in 42 countries and boasts the youngest fleet in the world, including 22 Megatop 747-400s. In September 1991 it became the first airline to provide a global inflight telephone and facsimile service, Celestel. Its inflight service, famous for its stewardesses known as 'Singapore Girls', is the envy of many other airlines.

Public Holidays
1 January: New Year's Day
*February: Chinese New Year
*February: Hari Raya Puasa
*April: Good Friday
1 May: Labour Day
*May: Hari Raya Haji
*May: Vesak Day
9 August: National Day
*October: Deepavali
25 December: Christmas Day

*Dates vary.

Disabled Travellers
Singapore Access is a guide giving detailed information and charts of easily accessible attractions, and outlining facilities for physically disabled travellers at public places and buildings. It can be obtained from:
The Singapore Council of Social Services, ✉ 11 Penang Lane, Singapore 0923, ☎ 6336 1544 or 6331 5417.

Singapore. The local currency is Singapore dollars (S$ or SID) and cents. Notes come in denominations of S$1 (being phased out), S$2, S$5, S$10, S$20, S$50, S$100, S$500, S$1000 and S$10,000. Coins come in denominations of 5, 10, 20 and 50 cents and S$1.

Banks: As one of the world's largest banking centres, there are nearly 60 international banks in Singapore. Official banking hours are ⏰ Mon–Fri 10:00–15:00, Sat 09:30–13:00 (some are open until 15:00). OCBC Bank branches in Orchard Road, Serangoon Gardens, Bedok and Yishun NorthPoint open on Sunday, ⏰ 11:00–16:00. Most banks change foreign currencies and handle travellers' cheques. However, some banks do not deal in foreign exchange on Saturday. Passports are required when cashing travellers' cheques. A nominal commission may be charged.

Credit cards: All major credit cards are accepted at big hotels (most small tourist-class hotels accept cash only), shops and restaurants. There should be no sur-charge on any credit card transaction and should any shop insist on adding one, you are advised to complain to the respective credit card company: American Express, ☎ 1800 732 2244; Citibank Visa, ☎ 1800 225 5225; Diners Card, ☎ 1800 292 7566; Hong Kong Bank Visa/Master Card, ☎ 6336 5277; Malayan Banking Visa, ☎ 6532 2604; OCBC Master Card, ☎ 1800 538 0118; OUB Credit Card Centre, ☎ 1800 221 7888; Standard Chartered Visa, ☎ 1800 227 7662; OUB Card Centre, ☎ 1800 253 6888.

Tipping: Tipping is not encouraged in Singapore as most hotels and restaurants levy a 10% service charge and 3% Goods and

Service Tax (GST) on customers' bills. It is prohibited at the airport. However, a gratuity may be paid to a service provider at your discretion if you are particularly pleased with their service, but it is illegal for them to demand a tip.

Official Business Hours

Mon–Fri 09:00–17:00; Sat 09:00–13:00.

Telephones

Local calls made from pay phones cost 10 cents for three minutes, with a maximum duration of 9 minutes. International calls can be made from your hotel, Comcentre at Exeter Rd, Telephone House in Hill Street, the airport and post offices with major credit cards or phone cards (available in denominations of S$2, S$5, S$10, S$20 and S$50) which can be purchased at shops and post offices. All the telephone operators speak English.

At Changi Airport, local calls from designated telephones (usually red or maroon in colour) are free of charge: useful if you arrive with no small change, and good for chatting to friends and relatives while waiting for your flight! Useful numbers: Emergencies: police 999, ambulance/fire brigade 995; operator-assisted international calls: 104; International Direct Dialling (IDD) access code 001; directory enquiries: 100; time of day: 1711.

Time

Singapore is eight hours ahead of Greenwich (Universal Standard) Time, seven hours ahead of Central European Winter Time, and 13 hours ahead of the USA's Eastern Standard Winter Time.

Weights and Measures

Singapore uses the metric system.

Water

It is perfectly safe to drink water straight from the tap in Singapore. However, bottled mineral waters are widely available from supermarkets and grocers.

Electricity

Singapore voltage is 220-240 volts AC, and 50 cycles per second. Most hotels will provide transformers or adaptors for visitors with electrical applicances of different voltage.

Shopping

Shops displaying the red Merlion symbol are approved by the Consumer Association of Singapore and by STPB. Retailers are encouraged to use price tags on all goods and to display a window sticker advising whether their prices are fixed or only recommended. Always avoid touts offering free shopping tours, special discounts or pirated goods. If you encounter instances of retailer malpractice, you can get full compensation through the Small Claims Tribunals. For more information contact the Consumer Association of Singapore, ☎ 6270 5433.

Tax Refund for Visitors

Bona fide visitors to Singapore can apply for a refund of the Goods and Service Tax (GST) of 4% which they pay on purchases of S$500 or more, at shops displaying the 'Tax Refund' logo. Goods must be bought from one shop or branches of one retail chain and must be taken out of Singapore within two months of purchase. Completed GST claim forms, with the items purchased, must be presented for inspection by Customs at Changi Airport on your departure. GST claim forms will only be supplied in shops when you produce your passport to prove your tourist status. For inspection of large items to be checked in, go to the GST Refund Inspection Counter next to Departure Entrance 1 in the public area of the airport before you check in your luggage. For smaller items go to the GST Refund Counter in the departure lounge after clearing immigration. Refunds in Singapore dollars will normally be paid within 12 weeks by the shop and will be sent to your address, or credited to your account depending on your method of payment. For further details of the scheme, contact STPB Information Centres.

What to Wear

To stay comfortable in Singapore's year-round heat and humidity, light loose clothing in natural fibres – such as cotton or silk – is recommended, particularly for walking around the city. You may need something thicker, however, to cope with chilly air conditioning indoors. An umbrella is an invaluable source of protection from both the hot sun and the inevitable tropical showers. Smart casual clothes are acceptable for most occasions, including evenings, though a few establishments may have a more formal dress code (check beforehand if you are unsure).

Language

Singapore has four official languages: English, Malay, Tamil and Chinese. English is widely used in administration, commerce and everyday life. Street signs and maps are all in English and taxi drivers usually understand it quite well. The language used between Singaporeans of different races is 'Singlish', a blend of English with Chinese and Malay. A few Malay or Indonesian phrases would be useful on an excursion outside Singapore.

Public Behaviour

You need to bear in mind Singapore's various laws concerning public conduct if you wish to avoid being fined for infringing one of them.

Jaywalking: Crossing a road within 50m of a designated pedestrian crossing, bridge or underpass is an offence.

Littering: A first offence results in a large fine; any subsequent offence means an even larger fine and possibly even some community service cleaning the city's public places.

Smoking: Smoking is banned on public transport, in museums, libraries, lifts, theatres and cinemas, as well as hair salons, shops and government offices. Many non-government offices are also non-smoking areas. It is an offence to smoke in air-conditioned restaurants.

Other: Fines may also be imposed on anyone who is caught spitting in public places, neglecting to flush a public toilet, or carrying durians or fast food on the MRT or into public buildings. Chewing gum is not in itself illegal, but it is an offence to import or sell it.

Gambling

Gambling is illegal in Singapore with the following exceptions: charity draws, Toto and Singapore Sweep lotteries and on-course betting at the Singapore Turf Club.

Safety

Singapore has one of the lowest crime rates in the world. Pickpockets and bag-snatchers are rare, and women in Singapore generally feel safe to travel alone. Nevertheless, it makes sense to take the usual precautions. Keep a separate note of travellers' cheque and credit card numbers and don't leave valuables lying around.

Dos and Don't in Malay Society

The Malays are steeped in tradition and custom and it is advisable to bear this in mind when meeting them.

• Always remove your shoes and leave them outside before entering a Malay home. Dirt from your shoes not only brings bad luck but is unhygienic as Malays traditionally sit on the floor.

• A man should not shake hands with an adult female in a traditional family: just acknowledge her with a smile and a slight nod of the head. Malays forbid bodily contact between unmarried men and women.

• Always use your right hand to eat or to hand things to others, as left hands are for more 'basic' purposes only.

• It is taboo and impolite to touch the heads of adult Malays.

• It is against Islamic law to eat pork or drink alcohol, so do not bring such gifts to a Malay home.

• When sitting on the floor, do not stretch your legs towards anyone. Men should sit cross-legged and women should fold their legs to the right.

INDEX OF SIGHTS

GENERAL INDEX

Page numbers given in **bold** type indicate photographs

GENERAL INDEX